Job Satisfaction
and
Work Motivation

Job Satisfaction and Work Motivation

Pranay Purohit

SHARADA

Sharada Publishing House
Delhi-110 035
2004

First Published 2004
ISBN : 81-88934-20-8

Published by :
B.L. Bansal
SHARADA PUBLISHING HOUSE
(Publishers on India's Past & Present)
2094/165, Ganesh Pura, Tri Nagar
Delhi - 110035.
Tel. : 30921560, 27552102
Email : bansal_sph@rediffmail.com

Printed in India

Preface

Job satisfaction is one of the crucial and controversial issues of Industrial Psychology and Behavioural Management of the world today. Though in a narrow sense it implies attitude of the employees towards the job, a comprehensive approach requires that many additional factors be included for a complete understanding of this issue. Work Motivation is closely related to job satisfaction. The present book is an attempt towards understanding the full dimensions of these two complex factors in the light of latest theories advocated till date.

An attempt has been made in the present book to understand this complex process by making case study. The conclusions drawn are startling and these are presented to the scholarly world.

This study, which originally constituted Dissertation towards award of Ph.D. degree of Bundelkhand University, Jhansi, was completed under the scholarly guidance and close supervision of Dr. N.N.Awasthi, Head, Dr. B.R. Ambedkar Institute of Social Sciences. The author acknowledges his deep gratitude to him.

The field work related to this project could not be completed without the close co-operation of Shri Ashish Dubey, Manager (Personnel), Raymond Ltd., to whom the author is highly indebted. Thanks are also due to the employees of the organization without whose active co-operation this work could not have been completed.

I am grateful to Dr. K.K. Sharma, Administrative Officer, Bundelkhand University, Jhansi for encouragement and help in various ways towards completion of this work.

Dr. R.K. Sharma, Retd. Professor & Head, Ancient Indian History Culture and Archaeology, R.D.University, Jabalpur came to my rescue in several ways to see that my thesis is given proper shape and published. But for the blessings of my parents and co-operation of my younger sisters, this work would not have seen the light of the day.

I am thankful to Shri B.L. Bansal, Proprietor, M/s Sharada Publishing House, Delhi, for kindly agreeing to undertake publication of this work and executing it within shortest possible time.

Pranay Purohit

Contents

List of Graphs

List of Tables

I
Review of Literature

Job satisfaction is the result of various attitudes possessed by an employee. In a narrow sense, these attitudes are related to the job and are concerned with such specific factors as wages, supervision, steadiness of employment, conditions of work, advancement opportunities, recognition of ability, fair evaluation of work, social relations on the job, prompt settlement of grievances, fair treatment by employer and other similar items.

However, a more comprehensive approach requires that many additional factors be included before a complete understanding of job satisfaction can be obtained. Such factors as the employee's age, health, temperament, desire and level of aspiration should be considered. Further, his family relationships, social status, recreational outlets, activity in organizations-labour, political, or purely social-contribute ultimately to job satisfaction.

In short, job satisfaction is a general attitude, which is the result of many specific attitudes in three areas, namely, specific job factors, individual characteristics, and group relationships outside the job.

There is great confusion in the use of the term "job satisfaction" and in the factors that contribute to it. Reviewing the many studies in the area almost leads to the conclusion that job satisfaction is anything that an author measures when he thinks that he is measuring job satisfaction. Too few experimenters in this field have been concerned with either the reliability or little validity of their measures.

Some studies have dealt only with attitudes on some specific job factors but have been called job satisfaction studies. Others have investigated other job factors and have also been called job satisfaction research. Still others have considered the individual factors and the job factors, and a few have attempted to measure parts of all three areas. It is no wonder that conflicting results are found in the literature on this subject. No study is necessarily more in error than another, but most are incomplete. For example, an organization that has a good personnel program and offers steady work, good supervision etc., may nevertheless find that a particular worker has little job satisfaction because of his capabilities in connection with his particular job, family problems or unhappiness or unhappiness about his failure in union activities.

One additional point must be made about the confusion among the terms "employee attitude", "job satisfaction", and "industrial morale." Although in many instances they are used interchangeably, they are not synonymous. An "attitude" is not "job satisfaction" although it may contribute to job satisfaction since the latter is comprised of a number of attitudes. Similarly, job satisfaction is not the same as industrial morale, although it may contribute to morale.

Attitude of an employee can be considered as a readiness to act in one way rather than another in connection with specific factors related to a job.

Job satisfaction is the result of various attitudes the employee holds toward his job, toward related factors, and toward life in general. Industrial morale is a byproduct of a group and is generated by the group.

Surveys and studies have been carried out on a community-wide basis, in specific professional or occupational groups and, of course, in specific industrial establishments.

HOPPOCK STUDY

One of the early community-wide surveys was conducted by Hoppock in the town of New Hope, Pennsylvania (1935). Eighty-eight percent of the 351 employed adults answered the lengthy questionnaire.

These results indicate that 15 percent of the sample had negative attitudes, or job dissatisfaction. This early finding is quite similar to the preponderance of evidence that has since been reported. Robinson and Hoppock have collated the data on 191 assorted studies reporting percentages of job dissatisfaction (1952). The median figure is 18 percent dissatisfied.

These figures are quite different from the "common sense" view in which workers are considered as robots doomed to dissatisfaction in work because of industrial mechanization and other self-attributed causes.

Hoppock asked 36 nationally prominent personnel officers to estimate percentages of workers who were dissatisfied. The answer ranged from 0 to 80 percent, the average being 49 percent. As Hoppock points out, if numbers from 0 to 100 were put in a hat, the average of the numbers drawn would be 50. Hence it may well be that the 49 percent is as void of meaning as chance itself.

The view that is clearly taken is that the majorities of the gainfully employed tend to have job satisfaction or are at least neutral. Only small percentages have job dissatisfaction.

Hoppock also conducted a survey on people in one occupation, namely, teaching. Five hundred teachers from

51 urban and rural communities in the northeastern United States estimated their job satisfaction on four attitude scales and by combining these scales, a measure of job satisfaction was obtained. Of this group the 100 most satisfied and 100 least satisfied were asked about 200 questions. A comparison of their answers differentiated the satisfied from the dissatisfied teachers in the following areas:

1. The satisfied showed fewer indications of emotional maladjustment.

2. The satisfied were more religious.

3. The satisfied enjoyed better human relationships with superiors and associates.

4. The satisfied were teaching in cities of over 10,000 populations.

5. The satisfied felt more successful.

6. Family influence and social status were more favorable among the satisfied.

7. The satisfied "selected" their vocations.

8. Monotony and fatigue were reported more frequently by the dissatisfied.

9. The satisfied averaged 7.5 years older.

One interesting finding was that the difference in average salaries between the two groups was not statistically significant.

One brief comment is necessary about this survey. No attempt was made to measure the proficiency of the teachers, and therefore it is not known whether those who were dissatisfied were less "good" than the satisfied group. This survey also brings out the point that job satisfaction and vocational interest are not identical.

In the epilogue to his study on job satisfaction, Hoppock proposed the following six major components of job satisfaction:

1. The way the individual reacts to unpleasant satisfaction.

2. The facility with which he adjusts himself to other persons.

3. His relative status in the social and economic group with which he identifies himself.

4. The nature of the work in relation to the abilities, interests, and preparation of the worker.

5. Security.

6. Loyalty.

Job satisfaction is an important generalized attitude in an individual, not a specific attitude about specific job factors. The idea that it is related to the individual's emotional adjustment suggests that those who are unstable emotionally may have considerably more difficulty in adjusting themselves to a job and may therefore be dissatisfied with it.

An excellent illustration of how job satisfaction is influenced by group variables is presented by Hulling and Smith (1964). They were interested in exploring whether men would differ significantly from women (in the same plant) in terms of their job satisfaction. They obtained measures of five separate aspects of job satisfaction from 295 male workers and 163 female workers drawn from four different plants. The data were analyzed with respect to the mean job satisfaction for the male and female workers. Analyses indicated that in three plants the female workers were significantly less satisfied than their male counterparts while in the fourth plant there was no significant difference. A test on the relative size of the differences was indicated across the four samples.

SUMMARY OF JOB SATISFACTION RELATIONSHIPS

In summarizing the research relating job satisfaction to job behavior variables, Vroom (1964) draws a number of conclusions, which are worthy of repeating here.

1. There is a consistent negative relationship between job satisfaction and the probability of resignation. This relationship appears when scores on job satisfaction are obtained from individuals and used to predict subsequent voluntary dropouts and when mean scores on job satisfaction for organization units are correlated with turnover rates for these units.

2. There is a less consistent negative relationship between job satisfaction and absences. This relationship appears to emerge most consistently with measures of unexcused absences, and when frequency of absence rather than actual days lost are used.

3. There is some indication of a negative relationship between job satisfaction and accidents. However, the number of existing studies of this relationship is too small to permit any firm conclusions.

4. There is no simple relationship between job satisfaction and job performance. Correlations between these variables vary within an extremely large and the median correlation of 0.14 has little theoretical or practical importance. We do not yet know the conditions, which affect the magnitude and direction of relationships between satisfaction and performance. Obtained correlations are appreciable on the occupational level of the subjects or on the nature of the criterion (objective or ratings) employed.

SOME GENERAL COMMENTS ON JOB SATISFACTION

Anyone who has ever held a job knows that if he does not get along with his coworkers the job is unsatisfactory.

The most rugged, aggressive, and independent individual will not be satisfied at work if he cannot get along with the working group. Furthermore, adjustment to people on the outside affects a person's adjustment to his job. A Secretary who is not getting along with her boyfriend or a husband who has had an argument with his wife is likely suddenly to find some dissatisfaction with the job which did not exist before; this usually disappears just as suddenly, after the "Kiss-and –make-up" stage.

In our culture, as in many others there, there is a strong desire to be approved and respected by others, especially one's friends. If an individual is to have job satisfaction, be must feel that he is on a par with his friends. College graduates consciously or unconsciously sacrifice money when they enter the professional rather than the business field. They are reluctant to choose selling as an occupation because they feel they are "too good" for it. The fact that eventually sells professional services does not bother them, whereas selling insurance or hats usually does. The factory worker whose friends also work in a factory can feel he is as good as they are; he will have greater job satisfaction than the factory worker whose friends are mainly office workers.

Job dissatisfaction may well be the result of a lack of vocational guidance. A person who is "too good" or "not good enough" for a job, in terms of his abilities and interests is not likely to be satisfied with his job. During the depression years college graduates were available at a "dime a dozen." Departmental stores discovered this and proceeded to hire them at almost this rate. But they soon had to discontinue this policy, because the young men and women were "too good" for the job and left in droves, despite the fact that there were few positions open. People are not capable of working for any length of time at a job, which they feel, is below them. This is true also of people who do not possess the necessary abilities. A college professor who cannot keep up with his students is likely to be a "sad sack". He may come to the conclusion that his students ask questions only to prove how smart they are. Certain police departments face the peculiar problem of having officers who are less capable than the patrolmen. The same phenomenon appears in all types than of business organizations.

Security contributes to job satisfaction, but we must remember that security is social as well as economic. More important, security is relative not absolute. Resignations occur in the civil services even though the positions carry tenure. Furthermore, some people holding these jobs report greater insecurity than some industrial employees who have the guarantee of continued employment. Of course, it may be that insecure people seek civil service jobs and that their basic insecurities prevent them feeling any great job security. Adventurous and dangerous jobs are sometimes considered "secure" even when life itself may be in the balance. A physician is secure in his position and cannot be prevented from continuing in it (barring a few legal exceptions), but he has no guarantee that people will call him. The point is that security is a relative, not an absolute concept.

Knutson (1952) makes the interesting point that what some writers refer to as security or insecurity is defined by others as adjustment or maladjustment, high or low morale, and the like. He states:

"Personal security is a 'dynamic' concept. People seek security within their various areas of striving by achieving it, they become secure in some areas; by failing to achieve it, they become insecure in other areas. The areas of personal striving are interrelated and overlapping, and some may be of greater importance than others to the security of the individual. Feelings of security or insecurity may tend to become generalized throughout the personality structure or they may be projected from one area of striving into others. Furthermore, the biological structure or physical or social environment of an individual, by limiting or influencing the character and direction of his motivations, may have a direct bearing upon the nature of his securities. In view of these conditions or possibilities, there appears to be a general level or status of security, as well as levels of security within the individual areas of striving."

A person's feelings of security or insecurity within any area of striving involve his own subjective evaluation of his success, in past and present situations and group relationships, also, his expectations, hopes, fears, or uncertainties with respect to the carrying out of his purposes and aspirations in future situations and group relationships.

Feelings of security within any functional area vary on a continuum, so that security status within any area of striving or within any situation may be considered a matter of degree rather than a matter of absolute.

Knutson found that the patterns of security of very similar occupational groups are more alike than those of more distantly related occupational group. This finding would lead to the speculation that job satisfaction may not be a unitary trail but that it may exist in some people when they are employed in certain occupations and not in others.

Loyalty is not to be overlooked in job satisfaction. The feeling that the worker has for his firm or boss, or both contributes to job satisfaction. Although it is not likely to be as strong as the "school spirit" evidenced by loyal sons of Alma Mater, it is present in employees. It is the factor that prompts service beyond the line of duty in relation to job requirements.

To understand job satisfaction better, we must take into consideration the opportunities for satisfaction that the job itself affords to the individual as well as the broader opportunities it offers to him. The job satisfaction index rises with occupational level. Kornhauser (1940) reports findings that have a bearing on this point. He asked four different economic groups seven questions dealing with personal satisfaction, and in each instance he found that the higher income groups indicated greater personal satisfaction.

Each of these questions is directly or indirectly related to job satisfaction. Questions 2 and 4 are the only ones to which the majority of the lowest income group gave favourable answers and yet they are of the essence of job satisfaction. This study is cited to show that if the economic range is great enough, salary may become a significant factor, but that with any one-occupation group (for example, Hoppock's teachers) or within a limited range, it is a minor factor.

Morse (1953) has published a book entitled: *Satisfactions in the White-Collar job*. It is based upon the interviewing of 742 clerical workers in a large insurance company. In addition, 73 first-and second-line supervisors were also interviewed.

As a result of this study, the hypothesis was advanced that satisfaction depends basically upon what an individual wants from the world and what he gets. Morse developed four indices of job satisfaction. The first is related to content of the job; the second is related to identification with the company; the third is related to financial and job status satisfaction; and the fourth is related to pride and group performance. While it must be stated that an author is as an author does, the point of view expressed in the text is to refer to job satisfaction as the resultant of the sum total of individual attitudes, and to refer to morale as a group factor. Morse apparently considers job satisfaction and morale as interchangeable concepts. To be more correct, she considers morale to be a combination of three of her indices of job satisfaction: job content, company involvement, and job status. However, at another point, she describes the degree of group spirit as equal to morale. While it is not important for present purposes to become involved in the problem of semantics, it nevertheless is important for an author to be consistent in definition as well as in application.

One of underlying generalizations offered by Morse is that level of satisfaction is a combination of both level of aspiration or need-tension level and amount of return from environment. Satisfaction exists when these two are in line, and job dissatisfaction exists when the return from the environment is much less than the need level of the individual. Morse found that productivity and employee satisfaction did not necessarily go hand in hand. This is similar to other findings of the Michigan group on section gangs on a railroad and factory workers in a tractor plant. All three studies find that high producers do not differ significantly from low producers in overall satisfaction with their employment.

Only one who is naive or who makes unguarded and unwarranted assumptions would expect to find job satisfaction and production related in a cause-and-effect relationship. This view is what might be called "unseasonable sweetness" – that is, all good things should be expected to go together. Since job satisfaction is a good thing and so is high production, the two ought to go together. High production, however, may be an employer's goal and job satisfaction may be an intrinsic quality in an employee. Many instances can be cited from everyday experience where people who are very job-satisfied are not necessarily high producers. It may be best to regard job satisfaction as an entity in itself, which may or may not be related to production just as one might hope to find that beauty and intelligence go together one finds that sometimes they do not, although sometimes they do.

Schaffer (1953) has proposed the hypothesis that "Overall satisfaction will vary directly with the extent to which those needs of an individual which can be satisfied in a job are actually satisfied; the stronger the need, the more closely will job satisfaction depend on its fulfillment."

Schaffer investigated 12 needs, using as his sample 72 employed men, most of who were in the professional and semi-professional occupational groups. He found that two clusters appeared. One contained needs that were passive or hostility restraining in nature; the other contained the assertive, aggressive needs. A high correlation existed between the person's two strongest needs and overall satisfaction. Among the strongest need reported in this sample were creativity and challenge, mastery and achievement and helping others.

Morse's work and Schaffer's work seem to point to the view that job satisfaction depends upon the fulfillment of personal need. Such fulfillment may not at all depend upon productivity as measured by the number of units turned out, and therefore the expectation that increasing job satisfaction increases productivity may be a 'Pollyanna' approach to the reality that does not exist.

Weitz (1952) raises an interesting point that a measure of general satisfaction of an individual should be taken in relation to that individual's job satisfaction. He advocates that a large number of job dissatisfactions are less likely to quit than those who have low general dissatisfaction. Other combinations are obvious, such as high general dissatisfaction, low job dissatisfaction (less likely to quit) etc. granted that we should know with what job satisfaction correlates. However, which we may hypothesize, we should not expect job satisfaction to correlate with arbitrary and assumed external criteria. We may expect job satisfaction to correlate with length of employment and production, but under certain conditions this expectation may be false. Both production and length of employment may be employers' goals and cited as measures of success. However, these two criteria are not correlated to any perfect extent with each other. Blum's finding (1940) that production and length of employment-correlated +0.44 would indicate that each is measuring a somewhat different aspect of success on the job.

Severin (1952) points out that care should be used in substituting one criterion for another since the median correlation of job performance criteria with various other criteria is about +0.30.

In a market of many jobs, the more productive workers may take better jobs and the poorer ones will stay on. Job satisfaction may be that the more productive workers, regardless of job satisfaction, take advantage of better job opportunities.

Whether job satisfaction is related to termination may depend to a large extent on employment conditions and the availability of other jobs. Therefore, the correlation between job satisfaction and termination may exist in one type of employment market and not in another.

Studies comparing job satisfaction with such criteria as termination and production may result in erroneous conclusions. It is necessary to be aware that many hypotheses exist concerning the relation between job satisfaction and production and/or termination or any other stated criterion. The hypothesis offered here is that job satisfaction can bear various relations to production depending upon a host of factors not usually even considered by some psychologists in their studies. For example, a correlation is computed as a result of taking a measure of production at a particular time. It is clear from studies investigating production that it varies from one period to another. In other words, production in the long run may differ from production in the short run and which should be regarded as the "truer" measure. If they differ, then each bears a different relationship to job satisfaction.

It is most important to establish what is meant by job satisfaction or dissatisfaction and then to measure it. If what is meant by job dissatisfaction is the number of gripes that a person has about a job, it may not be correct to assume that the person who gripes will necessarily leave the job. It may happen that gripper is competent and feels free to gripe, whereas the person who is unsure and is afraid to complain may leave the job because he is really dissatisfied. This again may be cited as an example or does not mean that this correlation would continue if any variable in addition to the two being measured were to change.

Research findings often lead to meaningful hypotheses, but they must also be mixed with reality. Many times the research will be stumped by the meaning of his results. All he has to do is ask the secretary or the factory worker involved to explain the phenomenon, and the answer will be forthcoming immediately.

Kates (1950) found that there was a positive correlation between scores on the Strong interest bank and job satisfaction in clerical workers, but he did not find that the expression of job satisfaction bore any relation to Rorschach signs of adjustment or maladjustment in these same clerical workers. He also found that the higher the score on the clerical scale of the Strong bank, the more numerous were the signs of personality maladjustment as determined by Rorschach respondents. This would mean that routine clerks might be satisfied with their jobs despite Rorschach's signs of maladjustment. This finding does not allow the generalization that routine clerks who are satisfied on their jobs are emotionally maladjusted. It merely means that the possibility exists that individuals may have satisfaction in one area in relation to their personality structures, and if these people were working in different areas they might have dissatisfactions. Thus, it is unsafe to assume that all "good" things ought to go together, and if they do not then there is something wrong.

Watson (1939) has conducted a few studies in job satisfaction, the results of which are summarized here to shed additional light on the role of salary as a factor in job satisfaction. He states:

"Without in any way denying the need of many workers for higher wages, it may be recognized that sometimes workers, vaguely dissatisfied with the way things are going, know no other way of meeting the satisfaction. They ask for more pay or shorter hours, and perhaps they should have these, but if these demands were attained, the relief would be only temporary. The underlying cause of dissatisfaction may be not in the pay envelope or the time clock but in the work itself."

Job dissatisfaction occurs when conditions of work and life are such that they block the gratification of strongly desired human needs. It appears that the phenomenon is more likely to occur at higher levels. The nature of the job and the reward (both physical and psychological) it offers are hardly adequate to gratify these needs (Physical, security, social and egoistic) to a desired extent at lower occupational levels. This may lead to a feeling of deprivation. Since a job is very much instrumental in the satisfaction of these needs, an individual may displace these feelings to the job.

Sinha conducted a comparative study of job satisfaction in office and manual workers by taking 100 offices and the same number of manual workers as sample. He drew the conclusion that "office workers group was more dissatisfied than manual workers. The causes of dissatisfaction were inadequate salary and not enough leave with pay whereas for manual workers they included lack of security, no advancement and the job not being congenial to their health."[1]

Raka Sharan conducted a study on working conditions and job satisfaction. Six aspects of working conditions were- wages, benefits, job security, promotional prospects, physical atmosphere at work place and social relationship with immediate bosses. He observed that the respondents got very low wages. They seldom got the benefits like casual leave, earned leave, medical or maternity leave to which they were theoretically entitled. They were dissatisfied with physical atmosphere. Their work duration almost exceeded eight hours a day. Workers mentioned that sometimes they had work without any break. Absence of proper lighting arrangements and electric fan at the assembly rooms had made the conditions still worse. The Researcher found that if the working condition show any market improvement particularly in wages, the respondent's satisfaction with their present job too is likely to improve considerably.[2]

In another study effort was made to find out the relationship between life satisfaction and job satisfaction and to study the role of objective factors such as pay, housing and other economic benefits in general satisfaction with life. Salary was found to be the most important factor accounting for 15% of the variance in the employee's perceived life satisfaction. Amenities satisfaction emerged as the second important factor accounting for 1.6% of the variance. The other factors that made significant addition to cumulative contribution of life satisfaction were active acceptance of norms, education and age. The rest of the independent variables including supervisor satisfaction, intensive job satisfaction with nature of job did not make any contribution to the employee's life satisfaction.

In India, Ganguli compiled results from three studies on Indian worker's ranking of various job factors that could contribute to the satisfaction or dissatisfaction of employees in their work.[3]

The ranking is as follows:

(a) Adequate earnings.

(b) Comfortable working conditions.

(c) Suitable type of work.

(d) Good and sympathetic supervisor.

(e) Opportunity to learn a job.

(f) Job security.

(g) Adequate personal benefits like Canteen, Medical aid, etc.

(h) Provident Fund.

(i) Opportunity for promotion.

(j) Job status and prestige.

(k) Good personal relations.

(l) Prestige of company.

(m) Free medical aid.

(n) More leave with pay.

(o) Clear instructions about the job.

(p) Cheap ration.

(q) Regular working hours.

(r) Share of responsibility.

It would be a mistake to take a merely humanitarian view to regard workers as a submerged group waging a commendable uphill fight for better conditions of life. The modern approach to the study of labour must accept certain things as a fact with no feelings of exuberance or regret. Secondly, correct answer to labour problems would require some understanding of the underlying social and psychological forces as well. While the economist can explain the probable economic effects of various measures and laws and can indicate how a certain programme may effect employment, production, profit and wages, the Sociologists and psychologists must analyse the causes of human behaviour and also decide what results they desire in a given context.[4] It is because of this reason that the need to undertake the present study was felt.

From the study of literature we find job satisfaction is one of the important factors which affect not only the efficiency of the workers but also such job behaviour as absenteeism, accidents etc. Work is important to men and job satisfaction plays a major role in general satisfaction. High job satisfaction is the hallmark of a well-managed organisation. Job dissatisfaction on the part of the employees may lead to industrial unrest. The main view of an organisation is to get maximum output of highest quality in shortest time period, with minimum expenditure of human energy and maximum job satisfaction. Satisfied workers are more productive than the dissatisfied ones.

S.K. Srivastava is of the view that there are a few studies on the measurement of job satisfaction with reference to different sectors in the Indian context. There are various intrinsic and extrinsic factors, which affect job satisfaction. The relationship of these variables in job satisfaction should be studied. Though the factors affecting job satisfaction can not be isolated from one another yet, for analysis, the researchers can, by the use of statistical techniques separate them to give an indication of their relative importance to job satisfaction. These days various organisations are spending on labour welfare and government has enacted many labour welfare laws so that the industrial worker is able to taste occasionally the better things of life, and so that worker is happy in the organisation. But whether these labour welfare activities have made any impact on job satisfaction among workers is difficult to answer.

References

1. Brown, J.A.C., *Social Psychology of Industry*, Penguin Books Inc., 1962, p. 86.
2. Raka Sharan, *Indian Journal of Industrial Relations*. 15 (4), April 1980, pp. 605-10.
3. Ganguli, H.C. , *Structure and Process of Organisation*, Bombay, p. 89.
4. Das, N., *Industrial Labour in India* , Delhi, p. 83.

II
Job Satisfaction and its Determinants

Job satisfaction is one of the most crucial but controversial issues in Industrial Psychology and Behavioural Management in organization. It ultimately decides the extent of employee motivation through the development of organizational climate or environment. Job satisfaction is a specific subset of attitudes held by organizational members. It is the attitude one has towards his or her job. It is one's effective response to the job.

Job satisfaction in a narrow sense means attitude related to job. It is concerned with such specific factors as wages, steadiness of employment, condition of work, advancement opportunities, recognition of ability, fair evaluation of work, social relations on the job, prompt settlement of grievances, fair treatment by employer and other similar items.

Job satisfaction is derived and caused by many inter-related factors. The importance of the various factors appears to change from one situation to another. The satisfaction, which people experience in their jobs, is in large part of the consequences of the extent to which the various aspects of their work situations tends to be relevant to their job related value system. Job satisfaction is basically an individual matter. Individuals look for those aspects of the job, which are related to their own value system.

The work values of the people, i.e. those values for which individual seeks fulfillment in their job have their roots in the basic need of the individual. There are not two people who have the same set of values, just as two people donot have the same fingerprints. The work values of the Individual take on magnitudes from the combination of their individual experiences and their cultural background.

The Executives/Managers have a central responsibility not only for the performance of other people but also of their own performance. The greater the satisfaction of the members to the job, the greater is the degree of effectiveness with organization.

An organization that has a good personnel programmes and offers steady work, good supervision etc. may, nevertheless find that a particular work has a little satisfaction because of his capabilities in connection with his particular job, family problems or unhappiness about his failure in union activities.

However, a more comprehensive approach requires that many additional factors be included before a complete understanding of job satisfaction. Such factors such as the employee age, health, temperament, desires and level of aspiration should be considered. Further his family relationship, social status, recreational outlets, activity in organization, labour, political or partly social contribution ultimately lead to job satisfaction.

In short, job satisfaction is a general attitude which is the result of many specific attitudes in three areas namely:

1. Specific job factors.
2. Individual characteristics.
3. Group relation outside the job.

These factors can never be isolated from each other for analysis. The approach, which seems to be apt, i.e. job satisfaction is the favourableness or unfavourableness with which employees view their work. It results when job required suits the wants and expectations of employees.

DIMENSIONS OF JOB SATISFACTION

Specific Job Dimensions:

The concept of a job is very complex. It has many factors, such as the nature of the work, the supervisor, the company, pay, promotional opportunities etc. The job itself seldom serves as a unitary attitude object. Rather, the attitude, in this case the satisfaction that the individual associates with his or her job, is really the degree of satisfaction with a number of different dimensions of the job.

Over years considerable time and effort has been devoted to discovering the dimensions of job satisfaction. The best conclusion to draw from this work is that although there are many very specific and diverse job dimensions that have been shown to relate to job satisfaction at one time or another, there is a set of dimensions common to most jobs that is sufficient to describe most of the predictable variance in job satisfaction.

"Locke (1976) presented a summary of the jobs that consistently has been found to contribute significantly to employee's job satisfaction. The specific dimensions like the work, pay, promotions, recognition, working conditions, benefits etc. represent those job characteristics typically used to assess job satisfaction. They are relatively specific attitude objects for which the organizational members have some position on a like-dislike continuum. They are also work characteristics salient to most people. Job incumbents quickly form very definite attitudes about the work they do. After very little experiences on the job they have definite feelings about how interesting the work is, how well they are doing and in general how much they enjoy doing whatever, it is they do".[1]

The general categories of job dimensions was introduced by Locke in order to cluster common dimensions into more theoretically meaningful groups. His system is useful for it provides some basis for considering the adequacy of the set of dimensions as well as a basis for better understanding how and why some dimensions are liked or disliked.

Singular Multiple Dimensions:

Should job satisfaction be considered a single entity or should satisfaction with each of the dimensions of interest be considered separately. The answer depends on the reason or reasons for being concerned about job satisfaction. If job satisfaction measures are used to diagnose potential problem areas in the job setting, then separate dimensions are more valuable than an overall measure. The Individual job factor to be producing positive and which one negative feeling on the part of the employees.

Combining Dimensions of Job Satisfaction

It seems intuitively obvious that all of a job's dimensions are not equally important and working condition not so; for others it may be the reverse. Therefore when combining measures of satisfaction with several dimensions of the job, it is tempting to weigh the dimensions by their relative importance to the individual. It is much better to select a set of job dimensions that have been found to apply to most jobs and then simply to weigh each dimensions score equally to calculate overall satisfaction. To have either strong positive or strong negative feelings indicates that the dimension is important enough to feel strongly about it. On the other hand, neutral feeling of satisfaction usually mean that the factor really does not matter much.

THEORIES OF JOB SATISFACTION

Job satisfaction is concerned with the feelings one has towards the job, and work motivation is concerned with the behaviours that occur on the job. Satisfaction is a hedonic response of liking or disliking. Also, it is often assumed that individuals will approach those things with which they are dissatisfied. There are various theories for determining job satisfaction for individual.

Comparison Process

The most widely accepted view of job satisfaction assumes that the degree of affect experienced, results from some comparison between the Individuals standard and the Individuals perception of the extent to which the standard is met. The amount of satisfaction that results is a function of the size of the discrepancy between the standard and what is believed to be received from the job.

Instrumentality Theory

A second view of job satisfaction is that individuals calculate the degree to which the job is satisfying by considering the extent to which the job leads to valued outcomes. It is assumed that the individuals have a set of judgements about how much they value certain outcomes such as pay, promotion, food or working conditions. They then estimate the extent to which holding the job leads to each of these outcomes. Finally by weighting the per received value of each outcome and considering all outcomes in set, the individual arrives at an estimate of the satisfaction he or she feels will come from the job.

Social Influence

Salancik and Pfeffer (1997) questioned comparison theories of job satisfaction and suggested that perhaps people decide how satisfied they are with their job not by processing all kinds of information about it but by observing others on similar jobs and making inferences about others satisfaction. In a sense they are saying that individuals may come into a new job not knowing how satisfied they will be with it. They look around, see others like themselves who are satisfied with it, and these observations influence how satisfied or dissatisfied they are with job.[2]

Social influence theory of job satisfaction is interesting because it recognizes the social nature of work and suggests a way of determining job satisfaction that has been ignored for a long time. It seems obvious that social factors do influence satisfaction and that they deserve more attention they have received in the past.

Equity Theory

Equity theory also contains a social element in which the individual compares his or her inputs and outcomes to those of authors. It predicts that too much of a good thing is dissatisfying. That is, receiving more than is equitable will produce less satisfaction.

Two-Factor Theory

Herzberg (1966) proposed that job satisfaction stemmed from an actively different set of causes than job dissatisfaction. He argued that "Satisfiers", which were such work-related dimensions as recognition, autonomy, and responsibility, and the work itself could affect only satisfaction and not dissatisfaction, whereas the opposite effect occurred for dissatisfiers, such as pay, work conditions, and human relations behaviours of superiors or co-workers. Both factors contribute to satisfaction and dissatisfaction, although satisfiers seem, in general to contribute more to both than dissatisfiers do. The two-factor theory no longer deserves consideration.

Conclusion about Theories

Of the five theories presented the Comparison Process theory seems to be the most important. That is they appear to explain more variance in job satisfaction than other points of view do.

Job Satisfaction and Behaviours

Is there any relationship between how successfully an employee performs and the degree to which he is satisfied with the various aspects of his job? The answer to that question is not yet clearly established. Vroom (1964) has done an excellent job of examining the relationship between job satisfaction and various aspects of job behaviour. Vroom categorized studies in terms of which job behaviours are correlated with job satisfaction. He groups them into studies of turnover, absenteeism, accident and job performance. In summarizing the research related job satisfaction to job behaviour variables, Vroom (1964) draws a number of conclusions.

1. There is a consistent negative relationship between job satisfaction and the probability of resignation. This relationship appears when scores on job satisfaction are obtained from individuals and used to predict subsequent voluntary dropouts and when mean scores on job satisfaction for organizational units are correlated with turnover rates for these units.

Povter and Steers (1973) also have the same view regarding job satisfaction and resignation.

2. There is some indication of a negative relationship between job satisfaction and absenteeism. The number of existing studies of this relationship is too small to permit any firm conclusion.

3. There is no simple relationship between job satisfaction and job performance. Correlation between these variables vary within an extremely large range.

Factors Relating to Job Satisfaction

There are many factors, which interact in a complex to contribute to satisfaction.

Personal Factors

1. SEX: In most of the studies on job satisfaction it is constantly shown that women workers are more satisfied with their job than men. The reason for greater satisfaction of women may be that they have less ambition and financial needs. In study job motivation has shown that a group of female prefer friendly people to work with, good social position.

2. NUMBER OF DEPENDANTS: The result of studies suggest that more the dependants one has the less satisfaction he has with his job, because much portion of his earning is spent on basic needs.

3. AGE: Studies have revealed that in some groups job satisfaction is higher with increasing age, in other groups job satisfaction is lower, and in still others there is no difference.

4. EDUCATION: The studies have generally shown that there is a tendency for the more educated workers to be more satisfied.

5. INTELLIGENCE: The more intelligent were highly discontented about the work conditions although physically it was the most ideal place to work in. On an overall analysis it appears that the relation of intelligence to job satisfaction depends on the level and range of intelligence and the challenge of the job.

6. TIME ON JOB: The study of "Sinha and Nair" showed that workers with service of three years and less and those with service of over six years were more satisfied than workers with service of four to six years. Thus it is evident that job satisfaction is higher in first few and then falls slowly.

FACTORS INHERENT IN THE JOB

1. TYPE OF WORK: Type of work is the most important

factor inherent in a job. Studies have shown that " variety of the job" causes greater job satisfaction than "routine work".

2. SKILL REQUIRED: The studies have shown that skilled workers have significantly higher job satisfaction than unskilled workers. Skill operates together with the kind of work, occupational status, responsibility, length of service, personality characteristics, opportunity to use skill.

3. OCCUPATIONAL STATUS: Occupational status and job satisfaction are related but not identical with each other. This is determined not only in the way the individual employee regards the status of his job, but also in the way it is regarded by others in the society whose opinion he values.

4. GEOGRAPHY: Geography has been found to have some bearing on satisfaction and dissatisfaction of workers. Studies have shown that workers in large cities are less than those in smaller cities and town. Worker's satisfaction and dissatisfaction cannot, however, be attributed to geography alone as it is inseparable from the working condition, the political, social and economic environment.

FACTORS CONTROLLABLE BY MANAGEMENT

1. SALARY: This is the most important factor of job satisfaction. Higher the wages, more is the job satisfaction. But studies show that in some cases salary was rated well below security and opportunities for advancement by highly educated class.

2. WORKING CONDITION: Good working condition are ranked an important factor in job. Better the working condition less will be fatigue and more will be job satisfaction.

3. SECURITY: The higher will be job satisfaction when there is a job security. But studies have also shown

that security is less important for better educated person.

4. OPPORTUNITY FOR ADVANCEMENT: Job satisfaction is more ebullient where there are ample opportunities for advancement.

5. BENEFITS: In studies housing, canteen etc. as one of the personal benefits has been ranked next to pay. But highly educated having a good pay give more importance to benefit and facilities.

"You can't eat for eight hours a day, nor drink for eight hours a day nor make love for eight hours a day. All you can do for eight hours is work." (William Faulkner)

Since Adam and Eve were directed in the Garden of Eden to earn their livelihood by "the sweat of the brow," man has found labour essential to the maintenance of his own welfare. Human life is surrounded by wants. A person satisfies one of his needs and immediately the next need arises. The man works only for satisfaction of his need. If all the need of a person are satisfied he will not work any more. For this the person wants to get satisfied with the job he is doing. For this many questions arise as to why do the people work? How can they be inspired to do better? To get answer of these questions it is necessary to know the values and attitudes of the individual. When an employee joins an enterprises and performs his duties, he wants to satisfy his economic, social and psychological need. When an employee does not feel satisfied with his job, negative attitudes towards the work develops in his mind. In this case he tries to change the job. This way, he finds himself unable in concentrating to his work. On the contrary, if an employee is satisfied with his job, he will perform his duties with his whole hearted efforts. He will contribute his best efforts to the best of his efficiency and capability towards the achievement of predetermined objective of the enterprises. A satisfied employee proves to be an asset for the organisation. For his livelihood labours some expectation are as follows:

Certain personal goals and objectives which will be fulfilled as a result of his affiliation with that organisation. Wages for securing food, clothing and shelter normally are his expectations, besides many other additional expectations. This expectation is universally true, for people work to attain their own personal, economic, social, and psychological objectives. The pursuit of these goals through work is both practical and traditional.

He has the right to choose to accept a specific job with a particular organisation because such a company will provide him a higher level of fulfillment of his needs and expectations. He in practice has chosen the job that brings him either the immediate or long range achievement.

The organisation employing the skills and service of a worker has a responsibility to fulfill his reasonable goals and needs. The worker sells his efforts and knowledge in exchange for certain monetary and non-monetary compensation.

Some scholars are of the opinion that the industrial productivity depends upon the productivity of workers because labour is an active force of productivity. This is the reason why great importance is given to solution of labour problems in the industrial enterprises. It is most important to develop the inspiration to work among employees, the feeling among the workers, that the satisfaction of their individual interest is associated with the achievement of organisational objectives of the enterprises. There are three schools of thought, and probably all are correct to some extent, which give little evidence in the available literature that employee attitudes bear any relationship to performance on the job: -

--First, there are some who assert that high satisfaction leads to high performance. The 'Hawthorn' studies of 1930's seem to support this view, as the findings of other studies.

--Second, others take an opposite view for example, Layman Poter and Lowler say that satisfaction results from high performance, because most people experience satisfaction by accomplishing some task, like building a radio, or clinching a sale.

--Third, still others claim that there is no consistent relationship between morale and performance. Vroom found significant relationship between morale and performance in only 5 out of 22 studies undertaken by him.

So some employees do indeed work harder when they are more satisfied with their pay, with the job itself, with working conditions etc. Contrary to this there are some persons whose performance starts because the incentive is gone i.e. they are satisfied with enough security or enough pay or a good job.

We have to understand values for the purpose of this study. Values represent basic convictions that "a specific mode of conduct or end-state of existence is personally or socially preferable to an opposite or converse mode of conduct or end-state of existence." They contain a judgemental element in that they carry an individual's ideas as to what is right, good or desirable. Values have both content and intensity attributes. The content attribute says that a mode of conduct or end-state of existence is important. The intensity attribute specifies how important it is. Values are important to the study of organizational behaviour because they lay the foundation for the understanding of attitudes and motivation and because they influence our perceptions. Values are relatively stable and enduring. This has been explained as a result of both their genetic component and the way in which they are learned.

Milton Rokeach created the Rokeach Value Survey (RVS). The RVS consists of two sets of values, with each set containing 18 individual value items. One set, called terminal values, refers to desirable end-states of existence. These are the goals that a person would like to achieve during his or her lifetime. The other set called instrument values, refers to preferable mode of behaviour of means of achieving the terminal values.

Attitudes are evaluative statements either favourable or unfavourable, concerning objects, people or events. They reflect how one feels about something. When I say "I like my job", I am expressing my attitude about work. Attitudes can be broken down into three basic components viz., emotional, informational and behavioural. The three basic components involve the person's feelings or affect-positive, neutral or negative about an object. Thus, emotion is given the greatest attention in the organizational behaviour literature in relation to job satisfaction. The informational component consists of the beliefs and information the individual has about the object. It makes no difference whether or not this information. Thus, emotion is given the greatest attention in the organizational behaviour literature in relation to job satisfaction. The informational component consists of the beliefs and information the individual has about the object. It makes no difference whether or not this information is expirically real or correct. The behavioural component consists of a person's tendencies to behave in particular way toward an object. Attitudes help in predicting work behaviour and help people adopt to their work environment. Besides helping employees adjust, attitude also help to defend their self-image. Attitudes provide positive or negative evaluation that employees hold about aspects of their work environment. The term job satisfaction refers to an individual's general attitude towards his or her job. A person with high level of job satisfaction holds positive attitudes towards the job, while a person who is dissatisfied with his or her job holds negative attitudes about the job. It is conversely, the stronger the belief harder it is to change it. It is easier to change attitudes when that change is not very significant by using persuasion techniques that is a positive, tactful tone, present strong evidence to support your position, use logic and support evidence by appealing to the employees' fears, frustrations and other emotions.

Job satisfaction is a pleasurable or positive emotional state resulting from the appraisal of one's job experience. According to Dale Yoder, "job satisfaction is regarded as the composite of attitudes of individual employees towards their jobs and relationship they create". There are three important dimensions to job satisfaction.

First, job satisfaction is an emotional response to a job situation. As such, it cannot be seen, it can only be inferred.

Second, job satisfaction is often determined by how will outcomes meet or exceed expectations.

Third, job satisfaction represents several related attitudes.

The satisfaction which an individual attains in his job is largely the result of the extent to which different aspects of his work situations are relevant to his job related value systems such as opportunity for advancement, job security, opportunity to use ideas, opportunity to learn a job, steadiness of employment, supervisor, pay, cooperativeness of the co-workers, working conditions, cleanliness, working hours, communication, recognition, individual adjustment and group relationship outside the job. If the job factors and the satisfaction they bring is perceived to be favourable to the worker, morale will tend to be higher than if the factors seem unfavourable. Factors affecting job satisfaction may be divided into two pars (1) individual factors which include level of education, intelligence, health, age, interests and family conditions (2) job factors that are nature of job, working conditions and working environment, stability of job, training arrangements, freedom to work, promotion, opportunities, effective supervision, proper remuneration, social aspects and human relation in the enterprise. The question has been often raised whether job satisfaction leads to performance or performance leads to job satisfaction. Performance results from the interaction of physical, financial and human resources. The first two are inanimate; they are translated into productivity only when the human element is introduced. However the human element interjects a variable owner which a management has limited control.

In fact, the level of the performance of an employee, is a function of his abilities and motivation. The first determines what 'he can do', the second determines what 'he will do'. Where there is strong positive motivation, the employee's output increases, but where it is negative or a weak positive motivation, his performance level is low. The goals of the individuals and the organisation can be achieved through stimulating workers towards productive performance called motivational process. It is a process of arousing action, sustaining the activity in progress, and regulating the pattern of activity or as a "willingness to expend energy to achieve a goal or reward. It is a force that activates dormant energies and sets in motion the action of the people. It is function that kindles a burning passion for action among the human beings of an organi- sation". Lawyer and Porter have developed a model that suggests that Productivity leads to satisfaction as shown below:-

Performance	**Rewards**	**Perception**	**Satisfaction**
	Intrinsic	Of equality	
	Extrinsic	In the rewards	

Performance lead to rewards and if these are perceived to be equitable satisfaction is the result. If the organisation wants to get work done by its employees, it may utilise a positive or a negative motivation.

Positive or incentive is generally based on reward. People work for incentives in the form of the four P's of motivation; Prestige, Promotion, Power status and Pay cheque.

Negative or fear motivation is based on force and fear or in a push mechanism. If workers do not work, they are threatened with lay off or demotion.

Extrinsic motivation comprises pay, promotion, status, fringe benefits, retirement plans, health insurance schemes, holidays and vacations etc. By and large, these motivators are associated with financial rewards.

Intrinsic motivation is concerned with the feeling of having accomplished something worthwhile, i.e. the satisfaction one gets after doing ones work well. Praise, responsibility, recognition, esteem, power status, competition and participation are examples of such motivation.

Self motivation or attitude motivation involves motivating oneself by setting certain objectives and goals before oneself.

Group motivation involves improving human relations and dealing with people in a human way by developing the will to do, by encouraging people to feel involvement in their work and by giving them an opportunity to improve their performance and by complementing or praising them.

Motivation techniques to motivate employees are

--Financial motivators connected directly or indirectly with money, wage and salary, bonus, profit-sharing, leave with pay, medical reimbursement etc.

--Non financial motivators are not connected with monetary rewards. In the words of Dubin, non-financial incentives are the psychic rewards or the rewards of enhanced position, that can be secured in the work organization. They are-

1. Appraisal, praise and prestige
2. Status and pride
3. Competition
4. Delegation of authority
5. Participation
6. Job security
7. Job enlargement
8. Job rotation
9. Job loading
10. Job enrichment
11. Reinforcement
12. Quality of work-life

Some modern theories stress that man should have control over his work environment.

--'Two factor or hygiene maintenance theory of Herzberg' defines certain characteristic tends to be consistently related to job satisfaction and job dissatisfaction. Employees, when they feel good about their work, they tend to attribute these characteristics to themselves. On the other hand, when they were dissatisfied, they tend to give extrinsic factors as the main reasons.

--'Adam's equity theory of work motivation' states that a major input into job performance and satisfaction is the degree of equity that people perceive in their work situation.

--'Path-Goal hypothesis' is based on the assumption that an employee's need is sufficiently great, sufficiently salient, and that he is free from barriers to follow the desired path.

--'Turner and Lawrencis requisite task attributes theory' defines task characteristics and also understands their relationship to employee motivation, performance and satisfaction.

--Hackman and Oldham provides 'job characteristics model (JCM)'. According to JCM, a job can be described in terms of five job dimensions, viz.:

1. *Skill Variety*-the degree to which the job requires a variety of different activities so that the worker can use a number of different skill and talent.

2. *Task Identity*- completion of a whole and identifiable piece of work.

3. *Task significance*- the job has a substantial impact on the lines or work of other people.

4. *Autonomy*- job provides substantial freedom, independence and discretion to the individual in scheduling the work and in determining the procedures to be used in carrying it out.

5. *Feedback*- carrying, out the work activities required by the job result in the individual, obtaining direct and clear information about the effectiveness of his or her performance.

Human being wants to work, seek responsibility, expect to know what they are responsible for and what is expected of them; and having participated in establishing the results they should achieve, like to be treated as mature, trustworthy people capable of directing and controlling themselves and then agree willingly to be held accountable for their performance, to be measured and assessed objectively. While satisfaction with working condition and remuneration is important, the motivated and creative input of people is brought about largely by providing satisfaction for them in their job, a challenge to their ability and an opportunity for achievement followed by fair recognition as a reward. That job satisfaction is aided by individuals seeing their part as the whole and identifying their own objectives and growth with those of the company and its progress.

The term job satisfaction refers to employee's "attitude toward his work environment. A predisposition to respond in a favourable or an unfavourable way to persons or objects in ones environment".[3] Job satisfaction is the pleasurable emotional state resulting from the appraisal of ones job as achieving or facilitating one-job values.

In the industrial context if somebody likes or dislikes his co-workers, supervisors, or reward system, it shows his job satisfaction. If his attitude to the above factors is positive, we say he is satisfied and if his attitude is negative, we say he is dissatisfied.

Job satisfaction consists of those outward and inward manifestations which give an individual a sense of employment of accomplishment in the performance of his work. It may be taken as a summation of employees' feelings in the areas which are directly or indirectly connected with job. It is the extent to which an employee is pleased or satisfied with the content and environment of his work. Job satisfaction and attraction satisfaction apply only to the customs already possessed and experienced by an individual whereas attraction is the anticipated satisfaction for the outcome.

Hoppock was the first industrial psychologist to provide the concept of Job Satisfaction. He defined job satisfaction as any combination of psychological and environmental circumstances that cause a person, to say- I am satisfied with the job.[4]

Some psychologists are of the view that "Job Satisfaction is an attitude which results from balancing and summation of many likes and dislikes experienced in connection with the job". While others are of the opinion that "Job Satisfaction is a general attitude which is the result of many specific attitudes in three areas viz. specific job factors such as wages, supervision and steadiness of work".

Study of Job Satisfaction can be divided into various schools of thought. The first being the Psychological needs school, exemplified by psychologists such as Maslow, Herzberg, Likert and others. They see motivation as the central factor in job satisfaction and they concentrate their attention on stimuli which are believed to lead to motivation.

The needs of individuals for achievement, recognition, responsibility, status and advancement are the stimuli.[5]

The second school devotes its attention to leadership as a factor of job satisfaction. Psychologists like Blake, Mouton, and Fiedler see the behaviour of supervisors as an important influence on employees' attitudes and direct their observations at leadership style and the response of subordinates.

The third school, strongly represented at the Manchester Business School by Lupton, Gowler and Legge, approaches job satisfaction from a quite different angle and examines the effort-reward bargain as an important variable. This leads to a consideration of law under which the wages and salaries of particular groups and the influence of factors such as overtime pay and the state of labour market and employees' attitude are constructed.

Yet another school of thought approaches job satisfaction from an entirely different angle and sees management ideology and values as the important factors. The kind of legislation formulated by management, which is the result of management's ideology, and the employees' perception of the legitimacy of this have an influence on job satisfaction.

Finally, some contributors, thinking on the subject, including the Herzberg School, seem to suggest that it is only necessary to identify the needs of the employee. The organisation, for which he works, must recognise his needs and ensure that they are satisfied. As such job satisfaction is positively related to the degree to which one's personal needs are fulfilled in the job situation.

Therefore, job satisfaction can be taken as a summation of employees' feelings in four different areas. Two of these areas encompass factors directly connected with the job (intrinsic factors) and the other two include factors not directly connected with the job, which are presumed to have a bearing on job satisfaction.[6] These four areas are:

(a) Job

Nature of work-dull, dangerous, interesting, hours of work, fellow workers, opportunities on the job for promotion and advancement (prospects), overtime regulations, interesting work, physical environment, machines and tools, etc.

(b) Management

Supervisory treatment, participation, reward and punishment, praise and blames, leave policy, favouritism, etc.

(c) Social Relations

Friends and associates, neighbours, attitude towards people in community, participation in social activities, social ability, caste barriers etc.

(d) Personal Adjustment

Health, emotionality, home living condition, finance, relation with family members etc.

Job satisfaction is an overall complex of attitudes that is generated by individual attitudes and factors inherent in workers and condition that emanate from the social environment of work.[7]

But some psychologists have rejected the concept that job satisfaction depends on individual attitudes. They are of the view that job satisfaction is more a function of job condition than of personal factors.

Feelings of satisfaction or dissatisfaction are complicated and varied. Working people may be satisfied with many of the conditions of their employment and still be markedly dissatisfied with other features of the job or of their working lives. The number considered dissatisfied will depend in large measures upon the arbitrary method of defining what the term dissatisfaction refers in the study.

Men work to earn their livelihood. They devote most of their life to their work, whether as managers, or workers, or technicians, or specialists. They spend a major part of the their lives at work and actually spend more time at work than at home.

On the other hand they have material and non-material needs. As soon their essential material needs are satisfied, they endeavour to satisfy their intellectual, spiritual and other psychological needs. In such circumstances, their attitudes towards their employment and, particularly towards their jobs, become important because their attitudes, as we know, condition the interest with which they approach their work.

Motivation of managers and workers is a dynamic force in the hands of management which, if properly used, helps to develop the human talent existing in the enterprise which, in turn is the foundation of the success and growth of the enterprise itself. For instance, consider the following:

Managers tend to see the weaknesses of subordinates and overlook their strengths. In any organization, they must decide to overlook weaknesses and stimulate strengths, and by so doing they can achieve productivity through motivation.

Motivation is the action that impels or urges an individual to assume an attitude generally favourable towards his work, leading him to perform satisfactorily. The action is generated by factors within and without the individual, which correspond to the satisfaction of certain material and psychological needs of the individual himself.

Motivational research is the study of the factors or incentives that stimulate people to assume positive and favourable attitudes towards their work and their work environment. It concerns the study of urges, drives, impulses, preferences, aspirations, etc., of people at work who, if satisfied, tend to promote and maintain high morale.

People believe that performance depends on competence, whereas experience shows that competence along is not sufficient to stimulate individuals to perform. Performance depends upon competence and motivation. Therefore, when considering performance, there is also need to take into account causes of motivation that lead people to perform at their best.

Morale is an attitude of individuals, or a group of individuals which leads them to co-operate in the accomplishment of a task.

Morale may have different meanings according to the context in which it is used. In the case of an organisation, it is the result of motivation. We speak of the "high morale" of a group which means that its members are satisfied, interested, co-operative, etc., which contributes to their efficiency. We speak instead of the "low morale" of a group when the members are unfriendly, disgruntled, unsatisfied and uncooperative which generally affects negatively in their performance. Thus, morale is used to describe an atmosphere or climate prevailing in a working place. Therefore, morale is the result of motivational factors or conditions created by management for the establishment of an atmosphere conducive to good work.

In research on worker motivation, productivity and job satisfaction, it is held that there are five elements which are important to individual, group productivity and job satisfaction.

They are :-

(i) The technical organisation of the group, which specifies the specialised activities that members should perform in order to get the job done;

(ii) The social structure of the group that specifies the values or norms members should share, of feelings they should have towards each other. If members A and B like each other and are willing to help each other, these feelings could help in getting the task of the group done more smoothly;

(iii) The individual task motivation, which indicates the willingness of the group to contribute their services towards achieving the purpose essential to the group as a whole;

(iv) The external rewards a member receives from doing the job in terms in monetary return, job satisfaction, job interest, job rank and status, etc., are usually considered to be most important to favourable performances;

(v) The internal rewards as expressed in terms of job satisfaction obtained from being an accepted member of the group requires sacrifices, for it is necessary to comply with values and norms established. In return they bring to each member, association, friendship, approval and support.

The Care of Managements: Rensis Likert, Director of

Institute for Social Research, University of Michigan, writing on Motivation brought out the following major conclusions:

"(i) We are consistently finding that there is a marked relationship between the kind of supervision an employee receives and both the productivity and the satisfaction which he derives from his work. We have found that close supervision leads to lower productivity and more general supervision, to higher productivity;"

"(ii) We have also found that employee-centred supervision not only generates high productivity, but more high levels of job satisfaction;"

"(iii) Books on management and administration tend to deal with the relationship between superiors and subordinates, between supervisions and employees as individuals. We are encountering increasing evidence that the superior's skill in supervision enhances is the productivity and the job satisfaction of the work group;"

"(vi) The workers belonging to higher production work group not only have greater satisfaction as members of group, but also greater loyalty, and help one another more and offer this help on their own initiative."

Most of the research work has so far been devoted to motivation of workers. Little research has been done on motivation of managers. It is probably assumed by a definition that managers have, or should have, good morale. This assumption is probably based on a popular belief that since managers are well paid (which is quite often not the case), they should have high morale. Experience shows that even when managers are highly paid they do not necessarily have high morale. On the other hand, high salaries or increases in salaries or the use of other financial incentives are not always practical. Besides salary, the following factors motivate the managers:

(a) **Organizational**

(i) Authority: It is the major attribute of an executive within an organization. Without authority his position is devoid of significance and his personality and activity prejudiced. The basic needs of an individual is to have a clear-cut job and well-defined responsibility and, as an executive, the necessary authority to meet his responsibility. There cannot be responsibility without authority. A clear allocation and definition of tasks is the basis of any form of motivation.

(ii) Leadership: Executives at all levels are also leaders and as such, should be encouraged to express their leadership through meetings, conferences, talks etc., with their own subordinates. Group leadership is essence of management.

(iii) Organization : Within the general framework of the organization, executives should be allowed and encouraged to make changes within their own units as long as such changes do not affect other units.

(iv) Promotion to Higher Executive Posts: Promotion to high executive posts is an essential factor in executive motivation. Vacancies in higher executive posts should always be filled by candidates selected from among lower executives and only in extreme cases should preference be given to outsiders.

(v) Executive Planning and Development: Executive development is another important motivational force. Selection and participation in management development programmes represents evident signs of management interest.

(b) **Psychological**

(i) Encouragement: This is a form of stimulation, which is given periodically to executives for expressing approval

and satisfaction towards results reached in executive performance.

(ii) Status: It is a factor of great importance in motivating executives, especially in larger enterprises. It has developed an extensive symbolism, which is expressed through different types of privileges, such as special office, private secretary etc., longer vacations, or some kind of allowance, or any status symbol designate.

(iii) Prestige: It is closely associated with status. Prestige chiefly results from the esteem and respect given to an executive by management, colleagues and subordinates. The status may physically express the prestige an executive enjoys within his organization. An executive may also have status but prestige does not necessarily follow.

(iv) Recognition: One of the strongest basic drives in man is the desire for recognition which may assume several forms, such as a compliment, a special assignment, participating in policy and decision-making, or asking his opinion on an important question etc.

(v) Healthy Competition: This form is used to maintain a healthy spirit of emulation among executives.

Most of the above-mentioned examples of psychological factors tend generally to stimulate a basic human urge commonly found among executives.

(c) **Mixed**

(i) Participation in the Decision-making Process: Practices and proceedings in policy and decision-making differ from one organization to another. Nevertheless, they have one thing in common: they always involve several executives. Prior to drawing or changing a policy or reaching a decision it is possible to call upon lower level executives to express their opinions or suggestion. The executive who is invited to give his advice on policy-making or on an important

decision will certainly feel encouraged. There is an added advantage in consulting lower level executives. Their advice and opinions are generally more realistic since they know and are closely associated with operational problems.

(ii) Top Management Conferences and Committees: They are often held for reviewing operations and discussing operational problems. By inviting an executive who is not normally a member, to express his views on matters discussed, will constitute recognition by top management of his value to the company.

(iii) Special Committees: Inclusion in Committees for examining difficult technical problem is considered as an indication of the confidence and interest management shows towards its executives.

(iv) Special Projects: A manager, especially if he has been in his present position for some time, is quite familiar with his task and has fully mastered his responsibilities. He may be a busy executive but his mind and energy could be easily challenged by new problems. The assignment of additional responsibilities is recognition of his capability.

Only positive motivation factors have been so far listed. There are negative factors caused by the misunderstanding and wrong application of management principles which should be avoided. For example, withholding authority from lower level executives is a negative motivational factor. Even if the executives concerned are well paid they will still be negatively affected and suffer from low morale.

Rensis Likert, points out that it is quite difficult to tell a manager that he is not as good as another or that he does not measure up to a desirable level of performance, without hurting his feelings. Likert seems rather in favour of obtaining correction from group performance, behaviour and individual self-correction. Among other things he stresses the following two points:

(i) People seek to learn new and more effective suggestions only when they recognise the inadequacies in their present behaviour.

(ii) People tend to respond positively to information suggesting potential improvements in their behaviour positively when this information is conveyed in a friendly, supportive atmosphere of a small, well-established group in which they feel secure.

Motivation of Men: The following are some examples of motivational factors, which concern more directly, the employees:

(a) The Job : The adjustment of his job is an essential factor in motivation and in promoting high morale. Although job security is a primary and essential need of an employee, especially where unemployment or under-employment exists, still the job should be sufficiently attractive to maintain the interest of the worker. The job should be somewhat of challenge to him. Training constitutes a prerequisite. Prior to placing a man on a job it should be made sure that he will be able to carry out the work in a satisfactory manner. Equipment, machines tools and materials must be taken into account to place the man in suitable condition to perform to his best capacity.

(b) Congenial Associates : A man adjusts to job but not adjusts to his team-mates. In such a condition it will be difficult for him to achieve high morale. Men are social beings and need to fit into a social group. Each man leads to feel that he is an accepted and useful member. Members of the team will develop high morale, if they know that their role is important to the rest of them. One of the expressions of high morale in a team is the assistance they give to each other.

(c) Leadership and Supervision : The man who is more directly in contact with workers is the supervisor. He is the

leader and they look to him for leadership. Promotion of high morale among the members of a team depends mainly upon the supervisor. Workers demand from him sound decisions, fairness and protection. They look equally to him to be treated with respect and dignity as human beings. He gives them recognition and security and keeps them informed.

(d) Leadership of Management : High morale and high output cannot depend only upon the employee and the supervisor. A supervisor who is constantly under pressure from management for increased output is not in a position to establish conditions favourable to high morale. He will in turn exert the same pressure upon his men. Therefore, management must exercise the same kind of leadership upon supervisors which they expect supervisors to exercise upon their men. The leadership of management reflects itself throughout the organization.

Many others may be added - fair wages and incentives, safe and healthy condition, opportunities of advancement, freedom from arbitrary action, consultation on methods affects employees etc.

(e) Economic Incentive : Positive economic incentive motivates for hard and efficient work eg. the use of piece rates, team bonus, promotion, etc. This economic motivation is more intensive pointed and within effective control when it is related to human capabilities and contributions. The underlying principle of economic motivation should, therefore, be to reward and compensate individuals or group of individuals according to and in proportion to their contribution. A man's contribution to an activity is manifold. The principal contributions are: (1) Time (2) Skill (3) Effort (4) Ideas (5) Responsibility (6) Working condition (7) Co-operation and (8) Continued services.

(f) Impact of Group Pressures : Even if the financial incentive is stimulating enough, at times the worker hesitates to earn that extra money if it is against the group "norm". In piece-work system it is observed that it is not the management, but the workers, who set production standards. When a new employee learns the job and works in a group that had set an informal production standard and if he surpasses the standard and earns more than his fellow workers, the group exerts pressure until he slows down to the accepted standard. The reason is that when a worker is member of a group, the motivational force of social approval exerts more pressure than the financial incentives offered by the management.

(g) You Cannot Hire a Hand : You cannot hire a man's labour without hiring him-the whole of him. You cannot just hire a hand. You cannot split the amount of money and when a man comes inside the factory walls he brings the whole of him along. You cannot blame him for this. He cannot help it. If all you needed was a pair hands, you would set your engineer to design it. But you need intelligence, skills and judgement which form a part of his personality.

(h) Non-Financial Incentives : There are several non-financial incentives, which you may experiment with to see their effectiveness. Some such incentives are listed below:

(i) Competition: Competition is a kind of incentive. If there is a healthy competition among the individual workers or group of workers, it accelerates their activities to achieve either personal or group goal.

(ii) Knowledge of the Results: Knowledge of the results leads to employee satisfaction. A worker likes to know the result of his job. A cobbler gets satisfaction when his customer appreciates the shoes he has mended. Generally the workers do not know the results and remain unsatisfied.

You generally inform the worker about his job only when you receive a complaint from the customer.

(iii) Worker's Participation: The importance of workers' participation is well known. This very programme produces many by-products, one of which is the enthusiasm it evokes among employees. Communication is like water; it flows very easily from top downwards but it needs an extra energy to flow upwards. Workers participation and representation in management need that extra energy.

(iv) Suggestion System: Suggestion system is a motivator, which satisfies many needs of the workers. Most of the organizations that use the suggestion system make cash awards for useful suggestions. They sometimes publish the worker's name with his photograph in the company's magazines and in their advertisements.

(v) Opportunity for Growth: Opportunity for growth is another kind of motivator. In this regard you will find individual differences. Advancement and growth are to some degree in conflict with the desire for dependable routine. To many people the security and things known and familiar are so important that the opportunity for change and growth has almost no appeal, while there are others who are so eager for something new and better that security means very little to them.

(vi) Fitting the Right Job to the Right Man: Production depends upon the interaction of the individual and the work situation. Fitting the right situation to a man is therefore an important incentive.

WORKER PROFILE AND MANAGEMENT STYLES IN INDIA

Man is the core of industry or enterprise. (Man here means woman also.) The success of any industry depends in how well-satisfied, contented and motivated are the man behind it. Just as quality raw materials produce quality end-products, "quality men" can be depended upon to yield quality results.

India embarked on a herculean task of planned industrial development with the implementation of the First Five-Year Plan in the fifties. With it there happened a sudden transplantation of the worker from the rural to the industrial soil. The inevitable result was a duality of root, and associated problems of absenteeism, psychological impact, need for extensive induction and training to meet the requirements of industry.

The present generation of workers consists of young men and women – born free, non-conformist in their outlook, rebellious in nature, angry and discontented- yet endowed with an alert and receptive mind and bubbling over with energy to try out original ideas and new concepts. The task is how to inspire these young recruits with the essentials of industrial democracy, so that when they enter the industrial world they can develop into useful agents of freedom, peace and progress.

Today, the worker is more educated than his counterpart of yester-years. His aspirations too are higher. He is more conscious of his rights too. He expects to participate actively in the industrial life. He expects the organisation to provide him with meaningful jobs and opportunities to develop and contribute to the best of his capacity.

The workers of today (and of the future) are more prone to get organised.

Changing Environment: Industrial Labour in India is a shuttle-cock, the rapidly changing environmental factors, summed up S.K. Bhatia as:

From	To
* Closed economy	* Open economy
* Seller Market	* Competitive market
* Medium technology	* High technology
* Tolerant society with modest expectations	* An assertive society with rising expectations
* Stable environment	* Fast changing environment

These factors have had great influence in the task of managing personnel. Major developments that have affected industrial labour since 1980 are as below. (It is not exhaustive, and can be supplemented.) The trends illustrated by these changes are continuing; and will continue into the future.

1. Apprentice Act, 1961

2. Contract Labour (Regulations and Abolition) Act, 1970

3. Employees' Family Pension Scheme.

4. Equal Remuneration Act, 1976.

5. Maternity Benefit Act, 1961.

6. Payment of Bonus Act, 1965.

7. Payment of Gratuity Act, 1972.

8. Inter-state Migrant Workmen (Regulation of Employment and Conditions of Service) Act, 1979.

9. Amendments to the Industrial Disputes Act, 1947.

10. Restraints in recruitment, such as through Employment Exchanges.

11. Recruitment from socially backward communities – SC/ST.

12. Social responsibilities towards handicapped and

ex-service personnel-preference for persons displaced from land and sons of the soil slogan.

13. Changes in social values regarding nucleus family.

14. Increase in employment of women and the number of dual career families.

15. Improvement in the educational level of the work force.

16. Increasing economic and geographic mobility in work-force.

17. Rapid technical developments.

18. Growth of professionalism in personnel functionaries.

19. Improved educational, training and development opportunities, particularly technical and managerial.

20. Implementation of "small family" norms.

21. Inflation.

Industrial labour in India has made significant strides in the recent decades, because of the increasing social consciousness among the entire community, assisted by a series of progressive pieces of legislation on labour matters by the Government. It is said that more labour matters are now covered by legislation in India than in any other country. The great speeding up in labour legislation since Independence is reflection of the urgency of industrial development and the determination of Government to achieve it in a few years, what it had taken other countries decades to build up by normal growth. Just as the pace of industrialistation had to be speeded up by expansion of the public sector industry, so the pace had to be forced in order to change the outlook of management on labour matters in accordance with the government's policy of achieving a 'socialistic pattern of society'. In fact, India has been able to ratify a large number of the ILO conventions, although she entered comparatively late into the industrial field. Matters pertaining to labour other than regulation of labour and safety in mines and oil fields are included in the Concurrent List of the Constitution of India and therefore, both the Central Government and the Governments of States have powers to frame laws concerning them. However, in order to ensure uniformity in essential matters, almost all important Labour Acts have been enacted by the Central Laws. The administration of these labour laws, however, is generally the responsibility of the State Government, who have been given wide rule-making powers to enable them to supplement laws and determine the details.

Industrial Management in India: The management of industrial companies in India has, in most cases, been in the hands of the managing agents since the beginning of industrialisation. The managing agency developed on the ruins of the agency house system founded by the ex-servants of the East India Company. The managing agents provided financial help, professional expertise, and acted as agents for sales and purchases. In 1954-55, there were 3,944 managing agents, of which 2,522 were unincorporated firms; 1,238 private companies and 184 public companies. These managing agents managed in all 5,055 companies. It was expensive, irrational and part-time system of management.

The system of management of companies by Managing Agents and Secretaries and Treasurers was abolished with effect from April 2, 1970. Alternate form of management with a Board of Directors, Managing Director, whole-time Directors and Managers took root. The reform was meant to separate the power to appoint and control management from the actual exercise of managerial functions and to foster building up of professional, technical-cum-managerial cadres, judged by their performance.

Many business families manage giant private enterprises. But, they do not have, in many cases, personal and family stakes of more than 10 per cent. A large part of the finances, both long-term and short-term, comes either from the public large or public financial institutions. The tradition of privacy accords the techno-structure (managers who guide the enterprise) autonomy for operation, compensation etc. The management here is free to optimise its behaviour in pursuit of the Company objective, within the framework of conditions imposed by law, practice and opinion.

On the eve of the First World War, the Cotton Mill industry was largely, but not wholly, under Indian Ownership and Management. The needs created by the War and the special object of reducing demands on shipping led to expansion of ordinance factories. Some associated industries and preservation of shipping led to expansion of ordinance factories, Scientific and Technical service cadres were proposed for management of industries, but due to opposition, abandoned in 1922.

The Second World War found India somewhat better prepared and equipped than during the First World War. The Indian entrepreneurial class exhausted its energies during the inter-war years in the expansion of cotton, sugar and cement. The leading progressive princely states planned and carried out a number of enterprises during and immediately after the war. However, the arrangements for their management, finance and marketing were not always satisfactory. There was tariff protection for many items; some of them enjoyed guaranteed markets, and various other concessions like free and cheap land, power, etc. British manufacturers continued to enjoy monopoly of supply of major engineering items to Railways; others largely controlled by the British, built up for repair and job functions, assembled imported components. Thus, although on the eve of Independence, India was one of the top dozen industrial countries of the world measured by the size of its industrial output, management remained in the hands of a few captains of industry, who were paternalistic, authoritative and autocratic.

Industrial policy since Independence has aimed at rapid growth of industry as spearhead of all-round economic development through a vigorous and strategic expansion of public sector enterprises, inducements for private investment, and simultaneous efforts to bring about institutional changes and social reforms facilitating industrial growth. Consequent efforts to establish a balanced pattern of industrialisation, to utilise labour-intensive modes of production effectively and to much social advantage, to compensate the ill effects thereof through technical and organisational improvements, to educate, train and develop the employees and accord them partnership in the running of industries, made drastic demands from the management.

The national economic effort is increasing Government investments in industry at an exponential rate over the past four decades and are likely to continue to increase in the same way in the future. The sheer size, extent and variety of public sector enterprises have demanded the deployment of managerial skill at all levels, quantitatively as well as qualitatively, far beyond that in pre-Independence era, and even in the first few years of Independence.

The public sector undertakings are contained within one ministry or other of the Government. The government creates the management of each particular undertaking within the prescriptions of the statutes which govern the undertaking. This may be specific Acts of Parliament, or the Companies Act. The public sector management is thus subject to executive, administrative, legislative control of the Government, besides technical and professional norms and standards. They have a problem to reconcile and resolve the expressions of involvement and concern of all these interests. As the complexity of managerial job outruns the practical experience and genius of individual managers, a management cadre imbued with the philosophy of the public sector naturally has to be specially trained and developed.

Management Styles: Style is something which all managers have, and which markedly affects the effectiveness of their management.

The Oxford Dictionary defines Style as the manner, rather than the matter, and defines manner as the way in which something is done.

Management style involves two things: First, it is concerned with the science of management which is practiced. When any thing is applied in a certain recognisable way, it is said to be a style. Second, it is a matter of choice--the choice between the several ways of doing things. When the choice is consistent, then a style becomes apparent.

Like many a profession or pastime, management has a scientific component in its procedures and techniques, and also an artistic component in the creative skill with which these techniques are applied. Without mastery of the techniques, it is not possible to practice the art. This knowledge and skill are basic. Also, it is assumed that the Managers have learned their jobs well. In their quest for effectiveness, the Managers use one style or another : good style gets good results measured both in tangible and intangible terms –that is, in terms of output, costs, staff turnover, and absenteeism; and in terms of co-operation, initiative, commitment and philosophy.

The study of group behaviour has established that leaders are picked to suit the situation. Management style is essentially a function of the situation and the situation here is defined by three things – the position of the company in its environments, the position of the unit being managed within the company, and the caliber and mood of the people being managed.

A great deal of research has been done on the subject. The most popular tool of analysis is the 'Managerial grid' which has thrown a great deal of light on styles. Blake's original concept was simply a graph whose ordinates measured degree of concern for results and concern for people. The original was called a 1,1 or "impoverished type", an extreme result-oriented manager was classified as 9,1 or "task management type", an extreme person-oriented manager as 1,9 or "country club type", an extreme in both as 9,9 or "team-manager" type; and a model of a balance as 5,5 or "middle road", in the center of the chart.

Blake and Mouton have described the five styles as follows :

1,1 Extortion of minimum effort is required to get work done and sustain organisation morale;

1,9 Thoughtful attention to needs of people leads to a friendly and comfortable organisation atmosphere and work tempo;

9,1 Efficiency results from arranging work in such a way that human elements have little effect;

5,5 Adequate performance through balance of work requirements and maintaining satisfactory morale;

9,9 Work accomplished is from committed people with interdependence through a common stake in organisation purpose and with trust and respect.

Each style points out the relative contents of concern for production or people. Blake and Mouton have developed training programmes that attempt to change managers towards the 9,9 style. Managerial grid is a useful device for a manager to identify and classify managerial styles, to help him understand why he gets the reaction that he does from the subordinates and suggests alternative styles that may be available to him.

Prof. Reddin conceptualised a three-dimensional grid, also known as 3-D management borrowing from the Managerial grid; and introduced a measurement of effectiveness to the same basic Blake grid. By adding an effectiveness dimension to the task-oriented and relationship-oriented behaviour dimensions, Reddin has integrated the concepts of leadership styles with the situational demand of a specific environment. These are his four basic styles.

The four basic styles result in eight types of managers--missionary, compromiser, autocrat, deserter, developer, executive, bureaucrat and benevolent autocrat. Any of the styles can be effective in some situation, but not in others.

All styles have an equal chance of occurring, a manager may use more than the style and no single style is suggested to be appropriate in all situations.

Three elements of style are personal impact, the medium for management and equilibrium meaning a dynamic state of balance, like that of a tightrope walker. Each of these components gives the Manager scope for deliberate choice. He has also the options of the types themselves, as well as a balance between leadership and bureaucracy, autocracy and democracy, innovation and stability.

Personal impact means the choice of the sort of person the Manager wants to be. There are only three ways in which he can make the personal impact, ie., communicate with others in an industry-by what is seen, by what is heard, and by what is felt. (Smell and touch, not relevant for industrial management). Specifically, the choice on what is seen covers, the dress, personal grooming (long hair, beard, etc.) bearing (alert, relaxed, smiling, sane, etc.) and appearance (trendy, athletic, intellectual, etc.). The Manager can be humorous, tight-lipped, casual and so on. What is felt really means response to the other people-how he listens, how he reacts, i.e. warmth, regard, patience, sympathy, or the opposites. Many of these will be reflective of the background, family, heredity, education, experience of life, glandular make-up, and the like. But, even with these limitations, some choices are within the Manager's deliberate control.

The choice of the medium for management is influenced partly by the same factors that influenced the choice of personal impact and partly by the specific channel of career experience through which the person has reached management level. In the latter category are specialisations, systems, sales, socialability, connections etc.

The dynamic state of balance is the more complicated element. It refers to the constant balancing act on a tight-rope which the Manager has to perform each day, with the point of balance shifting as the situation changes and with depths of different kinds of disaster on either side, if the balance is lost. Chief amongst these are the degree of different kinds of disaster on either side, if the shifting as the situation changes and with depths of different kinds of disaster on either side, if the balance is lost. Chief amongst these are the degree of organisation, the degree of participation and the degree of change. In choosing the point of balance in each of these, the Manager displays his choice of management style.

The degree of organisation is a choice between leadership and bureaucracy or between individual strength and organisational strength-or between competitiveness and equality. The leadership ends by the strength of logical imagination, enterprise and adaptability; the bureaucracy end by the strengths of logical impersonality of decisions, defined systems, stability and order. A mixture of both and a right mixture at that should be the choice. For, excess leadership can produce inconsistency, disorder, anarchy, amateurism, and instability. And, excess bureaucracy can bring about inflexibility, inertia, indifference, buck-passing, petty politics and red tape.

Degree of participation means choice between autocracy and democracy, between authoritarian decisions and participative decisions, between discipline and permissiveness. At its simplest, the options are--how much dictatorship; how wise is it to use the latter. The extremes are Taylor's Scientific needs of Individual Management (authoritarian bias) and Human Relations Movement led by Mayo (based on internal needs of individual) as well as Theory X and Theory Y of McGregor.

The democratic style has been shown by experiment and observation to be the most successful general-purpose pattern (save exceptions). It gives individual satisfaction, wiser decisions, commitment to decision, and some development of individuality in management decision-making. The weaknesses are narrow-mindedness, isolation, discontent, resentment, length of time required, uncertainty and unpredictability of behaviour and presumptions of staff. (At the other end, autocracy gives decisive action, speed, drive and because of discipline, predictable behaviour, once a decision is made).

The third balance is that of degree of change-between innovation and stability, growth and retrenchment, sophistication and simplicity. The strengths and weaknesses are that innovation makes for a progressive, opportunist company, which attracts and holds capital and good staff, but which can overstretch its resources to unpredictable products with high pioneering expenses and in the process, go broke; it can get pre-occupied with growth for its own sake and get unwieldy. Other advantages are safety, consistency and predictability. But, disadvantages are apathy, poor staff, retrenchment and even diminution in size.

These three balances dominate a manager's thinking in one degree or another and conditions his style. The choice is not between good or bad action, but between different kinds of good; in its exercise, any style would show its weaknesses.

The whole point of style analysis is to get better results through the training of the managers. Real improvements have made as a result of training.

Management styles in Indian industries:

Early Indian management has been described as 'family management' with traditional values. The distinguishing features are that both ownership and control of the organisation are in the hands of the members of the family and that organisational objective is to maximise profits, even if it necessitates exploitation of the weaker sections of the society. The manager is believed to be autocratic with subordinates closely supervised by their superiors.

In pre-Independence days, changes in the nature and dimensions of Indian business demanded that ownership and control be divorced from each other. Management positions began to be held by persons who have professional skills and experience. Even so, it was not rare for all decision-making to be centralised at the top with the head of the family, who had no professionalism, but perhaps only experience and intuition.

With ushering in of the era of planned economic development in free India, we began slowly and gradually moving towards modernisation and professionalisation of management, though there is still a long way to go. Entry of professional managers with academic training in managerial skills into Indian managerial scene was rather by compulsion than by choice.

Just as private sector managers carry a lot of family and business house traits, the public sector managers, being deputationists from the Government, often heavily borrowed the traits of bureaucracy. This is also changing. A.D Moddie (Indian Manager and his Environment, *ACSI, Journal of Management*, Sept, 1971) has portrayed the picture of Indian Manager as "his style in western, bureaucratic, affluent and aloof". He is a plutocrat in a poor country, a high class man in a class-conscious society seeking to be egalitarian. Socially and educationally, he has hardly any links with his workforce, with the trade. The Indian Manager seems to suffer from the social isolation of a high class and a different culture; he is too involved in the social responsibilities of a citizen and he takes the political environment for granted. This isolation is perhaps his biggest weakness and may well reduce rather than enhance his future influence in a society where he has an island of the "haves" in an ocean of "have-not".

Job satisfaction is one of the important factors that have drawn attention of managers in the organisation as well as academicians. Various studies have been conducted to find out the factors which determine job satisfaction and the way it influences productivity in the organisation. Though there is no conclusive evidence that job satisfaction affects productivity directly because productivity depends on so many variables, it is still a prime concern for managers.

"Job satisfaction is the amount of pleasure or contentment associated with a job. If you like your job intensely, you will experience high job satisfaction. If you dislike your job intensely, you will experience job dissatisfaction".

It is therefore necessary to discuss this factor in greater details.

Determinants of Job Satisfaction

While analysing the various determinants of job satisfaction, we have to keep in mind that all individuals do not derive the same degree of satisfaction though they perform the same job in the same environment and at the same time. Therefore, it appears that besides the nature of job and job environment, there are individual variables which affect job satisfaction. Thus, there are factors which provide a balance among individual variables, nature of job, and situational variables determine the degree of job satisfaction. These factors are:

Individual Factors :

Individuals have certain expectations from their jobs. If these expectations are met from the jobs, they feel satisfied. These expectations are based on an individual's level of education, age, and other factors.

1. *Level of Education* : Level of education of an individual is a factor which determines the degree of job satisfaction. For example, several studies have found negative correlation between the level of education, particularly higher level of education and job satisfaction. The possible reason for this phenomenon may be that highly educated persons have very high expectations from their jobs which remain unsatisfied. In their case, Peter's principle which suggests that every individual tries to reach his level of incompetence, applies more quickly.

2. *Age* : Individuals experience different degree of job satisfaction at different stages of their life. Job satisfaction is high at the initial stage, gets gradually reduced, starts rising upto certain stage, and finally dips to a low degree. The possible reasons for this phenomenon are like this. When an individual joins an organisation, he may have some unrealistic assumptions about what he is going to derive from his work. These assumptions make him more satisfied. However, when these assumptions fall short of reality, job satisfaction goes down. It starts rising again as he starts to assess the job in right perspective and corrects his assumptions. At the last, particularly at the end of the career, job satisfaction goes down because of fear of retirement and future outcome.

3. *Other Factors* : Besides the above two factors, there are other individual factors which affect job satisfaction. If an individual does not have favourable social and family life, he may not feel happy at the workplace. Similarly, other personal problems associated with him may affect his level of job satisfaction.

Nature of Job :

Nature of job determines job satisfaction which is in the form of occupation level and job content.

1. *Occupation Level* : Higher level jobs provide more satisfaction as compared to lower levels. This happens because high level jobs carry prestige and status in the society which itself becomes source of satisfaction for the job holders. For example, professionals derive more satisfaction as compared to salaried people, factory workers are least satisfied.

2. *Job content* : Job content refers to the intrinsic value of the job which depends on the requirement of skills for performing it, and the degree of responsibility and growth it offers. A higher content of these factors provides higher

satisfaction. For example, a routine and repetitive job provides lesser satisfaction; the degree of satisfaction progressively increases in job rotation, job enlargement, and job enrichment.

Situational Variables:

Situational variables related to job satisfaction lie in organisational context-formal and informal. Formal organisation is created by the management and informal organisation emerges out of the interaction of individuals in the organisation. Some of the important factors which affect job satisfaction are given below:

1. *Working Conditions* : Working conditions, particularly physical work environment like conditions of workplace and associated facilities for performing the job determine job satisfaction. These work in two ways. First, these provide means for job performance. Second, provision of these conditions affects the individual's perception about the organisation. If these factors are favourable, individuals experience higher level of job satisfaction.

2. *Supervision* : The type of supervision affects job satisfaction as in each type of supervision, the degree of importance attached to individuals varies. In employee-oriented supervision, there is more concern for people which is perceived favourably by them and provides them more satisfaction. In job-oriented supervision, there is more emphasis on the performance of the job and people become secondary. This situation decreases job satisfaction.

3. *Equitable Rewards* : The type of linkage that is provided between job performance and rewards determines the degree of job satisfaction. If the reward is perceived to be based on the job performance and equitable, it offers higher satisfaction. If the reward is perceived to be based on considerations other than the job performance, it affects job satisfaction adversely.

4. *Opportunity for Promotion* : It is true that individuals seek satisfaction in their jobs in the context of job nature and work environment but they also attach importance to the opportunities for promotion that these jobs offer. If the present job offers opportunity of promotion in future, it provides more satisfaction. If the opportunity for such promotion is lacking, it reduces satisfaction.

5. *Work Group* : Individuals work in group, either created formally, or they develop on their own to seek emotional satisfaction at the workplace. To the extent such groups are cohesive, the degree of satisfaction is high. If the group is not cohesive, job satisfaction is low. In a cohesive group, people derive satisfaction out of their interpersonal interaction and workplace become satisfying leading to job satisfaction.

EFFECTS OF JOB SATISFACTION

Job satisfaction has a variety of effects. These effects may be seen in the context of an individual's physical and mental health, productivity and turnover:

Physical and Mental Health:

The degree of job satisfaction affects an individual's physical and mental health. Since job satisfaction is a type of mental feeling, its favourableness or unfavourableness affects the individual psychologically which ultimately affects his physical health. For example, Lawler has point out that drug abuse, alcoholism, and mental and physical health result from psychologically harmful jobs. Further, since a job is an important part of life, job satisfaction influences general life satisfaction. The result is that there is spillover effect which occurs in both directions between job and life satisfaction.

Productivity:

There are two views about the relationship between job satisfaction and productivity:

1. A happy worker is a productive worker,

2. A happy worker is not necessarily a productive worker.

The first view establishes a direct cause-effect relationship between job satisfaction and productivity; when satisfaction increases, productivity increase when job satisfaction decreases, productivity decreases. The basic logic behind this is that a happy worker will put more efforts for job performance. However, this may not be true in all cases. For example, a worker having low expectations from his jobs may feel satisfied but he may not put his efforts more vigorously because of his low expectations from the job. Therefore, this view does not explain fully the complex relationship between job satisfaction and productivity.

The other view is that a satisfied worker is not necessarily a productive worker. Research studies also support this view. This relationship may be explained in terms of the operation of two factors--effect of job performance on satisfaction and organisational expectations from individuals for job performance.

Job performance leads to job satisfaction and not the other way round. The basic factor for this phenomenon is the rewards (a source of satisfaction) attached with performance. There are two types of rewards-intrinsic and extrinsic. The intrinsic reward stems from the job itself which may be in the form of growth potential, challenging job, etc. The satisfaction on such a type of reward may help to increase productivity. The extrinsic reward is subject to control by management such as salary, bonus, etc. Any increase in these factors does not help to increase productivity though factors increase job satisfaction.

A happy worker does not necessarily contribute to higher productivity because he has to operate under certain technological constraints and, therefore, he cannot go beyond certain output. Further, this constraint affects the management's expectations from the individual in the form of lower output. Thus, the work situation is pegged to minimally acceptable level of performance.

However, it does not mean that the job satisfaction has no impact on productivity. A satisfied worker may not necessarily lead to increased productivity but a dissatisfied worker leads to lower productivity.

Absenteeism:

Absenteeism refers to the frequency of absence of a job holder from the work place - either unexcused absence due to some avoidable reasons or long absence due to some unavoidable reasons. It is the former type of absence which is a matter of concern. This absence is due to lack of satisfaction from the job which produces a 'lack of will to work' and alienates a worker from work as far as possible. Thus, job satisfaction is related to absenteeism.

Employee Turnover:

Turnover of employees is the rate at which employees leave the organisation within a given period of time. When an individual feels dissatisfaction in the organisation, he tries to overcome this through various ways of defence mechanism. If he is not able to do so, he opts to leave the organisation. Thus, in general case, employee turnover is related to job satisfaction. However, job satisfaction is not the only cause of employee turnover, the other cause being better opportunity elsewhere. For example, in the present context, the rate of turnover of computer software professionals is very high in India. However, these professionals leave their organisations not simply because they are not satisfied but because of the opportunities offered from other sources particularly from foreign companies located abroad.

Job satisfaction is not the same as motivation. It is more of an attitude, an internal state of the person concerned. It could, for example, be associated with a personal feeling of achievement. Herzberg in his two-factor theory of motivation advocated 'job enrichment' to give people the opportunity to use their talents and abilities, to exercise self-control over their job and thus to attain job satisfaction. The other two problems confronted by the executives include alienation and stress among the employees. Both these affect the level of job satisfaction adversely.

The term 'job satisfaction' is commonly used by the academicians and the executives. In the words of Feldman and Arnold, "Job satisfaction is the amount of overall positive effect or feelings that individuals have towards their jobs."[8] "Job satisfaction is the amount of pleasure of contentment associated with a job. If you like your job intensely, you will experience high job satisfaction. If you dislike your job intensely, you will experience job dissatisfaction."[9] Job satisfaction is an individual's emotional reaction to the job itself. It is his attitude toward his job.

Job satisfaction is a complex concept and difficult to measure objectively. The level of job satisfaction is affected by a wide range of variables relating to individual, social, cultural, organisational and environment factors as stated below:

(i) *Individual factors*: Personality. education, intelligence and abilities, age, marital status, orientation to work.

(ii) *Social factors*: Personality with co-workers, group working and norms, opportunities for interaction, informal relations, etc.

(iii) *Cultural factor*: Attitudes, beliefs and values.

(iv) *Organisational factors*: Nature and size, formal structure, personnel policies and procedures, industrial relations, nature of work, technology and work organisation, supervision and styles of leadership, management systems, working conditions.

(v) *Environmental factors*: Economic, social, technical and governmental influences.

These factors affect job satisfaction of certain individuals in given set of circumstances but not necessarily in other. Some workers may be satisfied with certain aspects of their work and dissatisfied with other aspects. Thus overall degree of job satisfaction differs from person to person

JOB SATISFACTION AND PRODUCTIVITY OF WORK PERFORMANCE

The old view that a happy worker is a productive worker does not clarify the complex relationship between job satisfaction and productivity. It was traditionally said that high job satisfaction leads to improved productivity, decreased turnover, reduced accidents and less job stress in the long-run definitely established.

The content theories of motivation assume a direct relationship between job satisfaction and improved performance. The expectancy theories of motivation, however, recognise the complexity of work motivation and consider in detail the relationship between motivation, satisfaction and performance.

Job satisfaction does not necessarily lead to improved work performance. For example, from the results of twenty studies, Vroom found no simple relationship, and only a low median correlation (0.14) between job satisfaction and job performance.[10]

Porter and Lawler found that job performance leads to job satisfaction and not the other way round. They argued that performance leads to two kinds of rewards-intrinsic and extrinsic. The intrinsic rewards such as growth, challenging job etc. stem from itself and extrinsic rewards are under the control of management such as salary, bonus etc. Intrinsic rewards are more closely related to satisfaction. For instance, if a person performs well on a challenging assignment, he gets an immediate feeling of satisfaction. The lack of correlation between job satisfaction and performance can be explained as follows: If job holds little potential for intrinsic rewards, and if extrinsic rewards bear a very little relationship to the performance level of the individual, resultant connection between satisfaction and performance tends to be weak. In such a situation, management should do the following things[11]:

(i) Modify the job so that it becomes capable of yielding intrinsic rewards for performance.

(ii) Correct the reward system so that it acts as an incentive for higher performance i.e., higher performance receives proportionally higher extrinsic rewards.

(iii) In practice, there may not be direct cause and effect relationship between job satisfaction and productivity at lower levels because productivity is determined by outside factors like speed of machine, quality of materials, type of supervision etc. However, the satisfaction-performance correlation may be stronger for people working as professional, or in supervisory and managerial position.

(iv) Argyle suggested a probable relationship between satisfaction and productivity for higher skilled workers, or for those workers involved deeply with their work.[12] However individual differences cloud the position.

The 'average' workers do work hard when satisfied. But some workers may work hard in order to forget their lack of contentment, and others are more content when work requires modest or little effort as shown below.

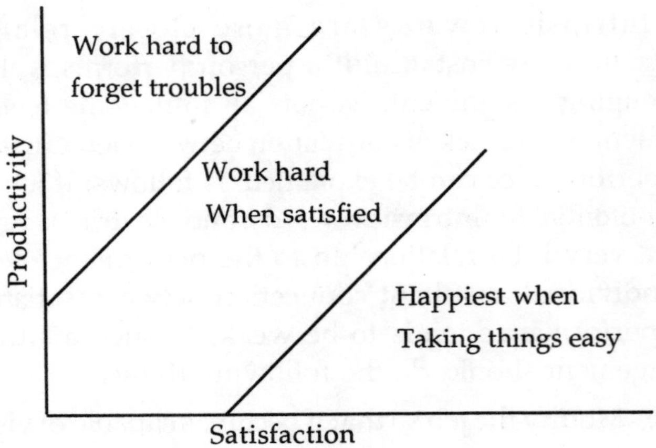

Thus, the relationship between job satisfaction and performance is an issue of continuing debate and controversy. However, three distinct points of view have emerged: Satisfaction leads to performance, a view associated with the early human relations approach.

(i) The relationship between satisfaction and performance is moderated by number of variables, a view that is reflected in research studies.

(ii) A more recent view that performance leads to satisfaction.[13]

Argyle also examined the relationship between job satisfaction and absenteeism and labour turnover. Both are affected by factors other than job satisfaction, but it is concluded that there is a lower level of voluntary absenteeism and of labour turnover, when there is a high level of job satisfaction.

References

1. Ernest J. McCormick and Daniel Ilgen, "*Industrial psychology*", New Delhi, pp. 303 - 309.
2. Ernest J. McCormick and Daniel Ilgen, " *Industrial psychology*", 1987 edition, New Delhi, pp. 303-309.
3. Steers and Perter, *Journal of Applied Psychology*, Vol. 76, p. 251.
4. Hoppock, *Job Satisfaction*, New York, 1935.
5. Bhatia, S.K., *Personnel Management and Industrial Relations*, New Delhi, 1983, p. 140.
6. Pestonjee, D.M., *Organisational Structure and Job Attitudes*,1973.
7. Sinha D., Job Satisfaction in Office and Manual Workers, *Indian Journal of social Work* : Vol. 9, pp. 39-46.
8. Feldman, D.C. and Arnold, H.J., *Managing Individual and Group Behaviour in Organisations*, New York, 1983, p. 192.
9. Andrew, J. DuBrins, *The Practice of Supervision*, New Delhi, 1988, p. 58.
10. Vroom,Victor H., *Work and Motivation*, New York, 1964.
11. Porter, L.W. and Lawler, E.E., *Management Attitudes and Performance*, Homewood, III., 1968, pp. 12-13.
12. Argyle, M., *The Social Psychology of Work*, Oxford, 1974, pp. 238-39.
13. Luthans, Fred, *Organizational Behaviour*, New York, 1989.

III

Work Motivation

Motivation is a general term applying to the entire class of drives, desires, needs, wishes, and similar forces. To say that managers motivate their subordinates is to say that they do those things which they hope will satisfy these drives and induce the subordinates to act in a desired manner.

The Need-Want-Satisfaction Chain

It is possible, then, to look at motivation as involving a chain reaction: Felt needs give rise to wants or goals sought, which cause tensions (that is, unfulfilled desires), which give rise to actions toward achieving goals, which finally result in satisfying actions.

The chain explanation is complex. In the first place, except for physiological needs, such as hunger, needs are not independent of a person's environment. Many physiological needs, however, are stimulated by environmental factors. The smell of food may cause hunger, a low thermometer reading may cause chills, or the sight of a cold drink may cause an overwhelming thirst. Environment has a major influence on our perception of secondary needs. The promotion of a colleague may kindle one's desire for a higher position. A challenging problem may meet one's desire to accomplish something by solving it. A congenial social group may increase one's need for affiliation; and, of course, being alone more than one wants to be can give a strong motivation for wanting to be with people.

In the second place, the need-want-satisfaction chain does not always operate as simply as portrayed. Needs do cause behaviour, but needs also may result from behaviour. Satisfying one need may lead to a desire to satisfy more needs. For example, a person's need for accomplishment may be made keener by the satisfaction gained from achieving a desired goal or it may be dulled by failure. The one-way nature of the chain has also been challenged by the work of some biological scientists who have found that needs are not always the cause of human behaviour but may be a result of it. In other words, behaviour is often what people do and not and why they do it.

Complexity of Motivation

It takes only a moment's thought to realize that at any given time, an individual's motives may be quite complex and often conflicting. A person may be motivated by a desire for economic goods and services (groceries, a better house, a new car, or a trip), and even these desires may be complex and conflicting (should one buy a new house or a new car?). At the same time an individual may want self-esteem, status, a feeling of accomplishment, or relaxation (who has not felt a conflict between the time demands of a job and the desire to play golf or go to a movie?).

Motivators are things which induce an individual to perform. While motivations reflect wants, motivators are the identified rewards, or incentives, that sharpen the drive to satisfy these wants. They are also the means by which conflicting needs may be reconciled or one need heightened so that it will be given priority over another.

A manager can do much to sharpen motives by establishing an environment favourable to certain drives. For example, people in a business which has developed a reputation for excellence and high quality tend to be motivated to contribute to this reputation. Similarly, the environment of a business in which managerial performance is effective and efficient tends to breed a desire for high-quality management among most, or all, managers and personnel.

A motivator, then, is something that influences an individual's behaviour. It makes a difference in what a person will do. Obviously, in any organized enterprise, managers must be concerned about motivators and also inventive in their use. People can often satisfy their wants in a variety of ways. A person can, for example, satisfy a desire for affiliation by being active in a social club rather than in a business, meet economic needs by performing a job just well enough to get by, or satisfy status needs by spending time working for a political party. What a manager must do, of course, is use those motivators which will lead people to perform effectively for the enterprise that employs them. No manager can expect to hire the whole person, since people always have desires and drives outside the enterprise. But if a company or any other kind of enterprise is to be efficient and successful, enough of every person's drives must be stimulated and satisfied to ensure effective performance.

Motivation refers to the drive and effort to satisfy a want or goal. Satisfaction refers to the contentment experienced when a want is satisfied. In other words, motivation implies a drive toward an outcome, and satisfaction is the outcome already experienced.

From a management point of view then, a person might have high job satisfaction but a low level of motivation for the job, or the reverse might be true. Understandably, the probability exists that highly motivated persons with low job satisfaction will look for other positions. Likewise, people who find their positions rewarding but are being paid considerably less than they desire or think they deserve will probably search for other jobs.

MOTIVATION : THE CARROT AND THE STICK

The various leading theories of motivation and motivators seldom make reference to the carrot and the stick. This metaphor relates, of course, to the use of rewards and penalties in order to induce desired behaviour. It comes from the old story that to make a donkey move, one must put a carrot in front of him or grab him with a stick from behind.

Despite all the research on and theories of motivation that have come to there fore in recent years, reward and punishment are still considered strong motivators. For centuries, however, they were too often thought of as the only forces that could motivate people. As the succeeding sections will explain, there are many other motivators.

At the same time, in all theories of motivation, the inducements of some kind of "carrot" are recognized. Often this is money in the form of pay or bonuses. Even though money is not the only motivating force, it has been and will continue to be an important one. The trouble with the "money" carrot" approach is that too often everyone gets a carrot, regardless of performance, through such practices as salary increases and promotion by seniority, automatic "merit" increases, and executive bonuses not based on individual manager performance. It is as simple as this: If a person put a donkey in a pen full of carrots and then stood outside with a carrot, would the donkey be encouraged to come out of the pen?

The "stick", in the form of fear- fear of loss of job, loss of income, reduction of bonus, demotion, or some other penalty - has been and continues to be a strong motivator. Yet it is admittedly not the best kind. It often gives rise to defensive behaviour, such as union organization, poor-quality work, executive indifference, failure of a manager to take any risks in decision making, or even dishonesty. But fear of penalty cannot be overlooked. Whether managers are first-level supervisors or chief executives, the power of their position to give or withhold rewards or impose penalties of various kinds gives them an ability to control, to a very great extent, the economic and social well-being of their subordinates. It is hardly a wonder that many subordinates are "yes-sayers", simply agreeing with their superiors rather than using their considered judgment.

THE HIERARCHY OF NEEDS THEORY

One of the most widely mentioned theories of motivation is the hierarchy of needs theory put forth by psychologist Abraham Maslow. Maslow saw human needs in the form of a hierarchy, ascending from the lowest to the highest, and he concluded that when one set of needs is satisfied, this kind of need ceases to be a motivator.

The Needs Hierarchy

The basic human needs placed by Maslow in an ascending order of importance are:

1. *Physiological needs* :

These are the basic needs for sustaining human life itself, such as food, water, warmth, shelter, and sleep. Maslow took the position that until these needs are satisfied to the degree necessary to maintain life, other needs will not motivate people.

2. *Security, or safety needs* :

These are the needs to be free of physical danger and of the fear of losing a job, property, food, or shelter.

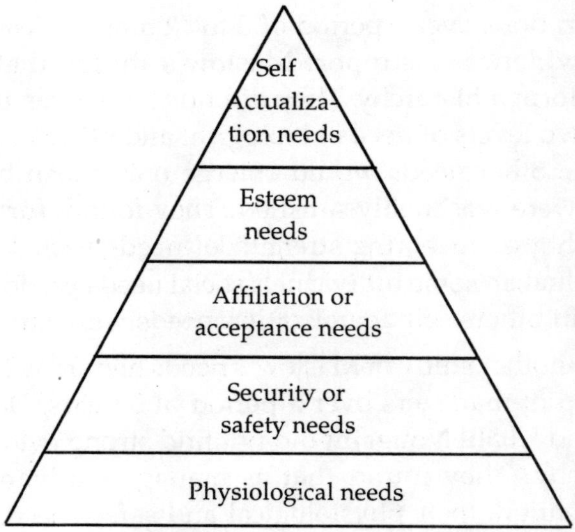

MASLOW'S HIERARCHY OF NEEDS

3. *Affiliation or acceptance needs :*

Since people are social beings, they need to belong, to be accepted by others.

4. *Esteem needs:*

According to Maslow, once people begin to satisfy their need to belong, they tend to want to be held in esteem both by themselves and by others. This kind of need produces such satisfactions as power, prestige, status, and self-confidence.

5. *Need for self-actualization:*

Maslow regards this as the highest need in his hierarchy. It is the desire to become what one is capable of becoming - to maximize one's potential and to accomplish something.

Maslow's concept of a hierarchy of needs has been subjected to considerable research. Edward Lawler and J. Lloyd Suttle collected data on 187 managers in two different organizations over a period of 6 to 12 months. They found little evidence to support Maslow's theory that human needs form a hierarchy. They did note, however, that there were two levels of needs - biological and other needs - and that the other needs would emerge only when biological needs were reasonably satisfied. They found, further, that at the higher level, the strength of needs varied with the individual; in some individuals social needs predominated, while in others self-actualization needs were strongest.

In another study of Maslow's needs hierarchy involving a group of managers over a period of 5 years, Douglas T. Hall and Khalil Nougaim did not find strong evidence of a hierarchy. They found that as managers advance in an organization, their physiological and safety needs tend to decrease in importance and their needs for affiliation, esteem, and self-actualization tend to increase. They insisted, however, that the upward movement of need prominence resulted from upward career changes and not from the satisfaction of lower-order needs.

The Motivation-Hygiene Approach to Motivation

Maslow's need approach has been considerably modified by Frederick Herzberg and his associates. Their research purports to find a two-factor theory of motivation. In one group of needs are such things as company policy and administration, supervision, working conditions, interpersonal relations, salary, status, job security, and personal life. These were found by Herzberg and his associates to be only dissatisfiers and not motivators. In other words, if they exist in a work environment in high quantity and quality, they yield no dissatisfaction. Their existence does not motivate in the sense of yielding satisfaction; their lack of existence would, however, result in dissatisfaction. Herzberg called them *maintenance, hygiene,* or *job context factors.*

In the second group, Herzberg listed certain satisfiers - and therefore motivators - all related to *job content*. They include achievement, recognition, challenging work, advancement, and growth in the job. Their existence will yield feelings of satisfaction or no satisfaction (not dissatisfaction). The satisfiers and dissatisfiers identified by Herzberg are similar to the factors suggested by Maslow.

The first group of factors (the dissatisfiers) will not motivate people in an organization; yet they must be present, or dissatisfaction will arise. The second group, or the job content factors, Herzberg found to be the real motivators because they have the potential of yielding a sense of satisfaction. Clearly, if this theory of motivation is sound, managers must give considerable attention to upgrading job content.

The Herzberg research has not gone unchallenged. Some researchers question Herzberg's methods, saying that his investigation methods tended to prejudice his results. For example, the well-known tendency of people to attribute good results to their own efforts and to blame others for poor results is thought to have prejudiced Herzberg's findings. Other researchers, not following his methods, have arrived at conclusions that do not support Herzberg's theory.

THE EXPECTANCY THEORY OF MOTIVATION

Another approach, one that many believe goes far in explaining how people are motivated, is the expectancy theory. One of the leaders in advancing and explaining this theory is the psychologist Victor H. Vroom. He holds that people will be motivated to do things to reach a goal if they believe in the worth of that goal and if they can see that what they do will help them in achieving it. The Expectancy Theory of Motivation is a complex, more encompassing model of motivation than equity theory. Over the years since its original formulation, the theory's scope and complexity have continued to grow.

The Basic Expectancy Model

The basic expectancy theory model emerged from the work of Edward Tolman and Kurt Lewin.Victor Vroom, however, is generally credited with first applying this theory to motivation in the workplace. The theory attempts to determine how individuals choose among alternative behaviours. Its premise is that motivation depends on how much we want something and how likely we think we are to get it. The following simple example illustrates this premise.

Suppose a recent college graduate is looking for her first managerial job. While scanning the want ads, she sees that Exxon is seeking a new executive vice president to oversee its foreign operations. The starting salary is Rs. 300,000. The student would love the job, but she does not bother to apply because she recognizes that she has no chance of getting it. Continuing on, she sees a position that involves scraping bubble gum from underneath desks in college classroom buildings. The starting salary is Rs. 3.50 an hour, and no experience is necessary. Again, however, the student is unlikely to apply; even though she thinks she could get the job, she does not want it. Then she comes across an advertisement for a management training position with a large company. No experience is necessary, the primary. requirement is a college degree, and the starting salary is Rs. 25,000. She will probably apply for this position because she wants *it* and because she thinks she has a reasonable chance of getting it.

The model's general components are effort (the result of motivation), performance, and outcomes. (Performance is considered a joint function of effort, environment, and ability. Expectancy theory emphasizes the linkages among these elements, which are described as expectancies and valences.

Effort-to-Performance Expectancy:

The effort-to-performance expectancy is the perceived probability that effort will lead to performance. In a person who believes his or her effort will lead to higher performance, this expectancy is very strong-perhaps approaching 1.0, where 1.0 equals absolute certainty that the outcome will occur. In a person who believes his or her performance will be the same no matter how much effort is made, the expectancy is very low-close to 0, where 0 equals absolutely no chance that the outcome will occur. The person who thinks there is a moderate relationship between effort and performance has an expectancy somewhere between 1.0 and 0.

Performance-to-Outcome Expectancy :

The performance -to-outcome expectancy is a person's perception of the probability that performance will lead to certain other outcomes. If a person thinks a high performer is certain to get a pay raise, this expectancy is close to 1.0. At the other extreme, a person who believes raises are entirely independent of performance has an expectancy close to 0. Finally, if a person thinks performance has some bearing on the prospects for a pay raise, his or her expectancy is somewhere between 1.0 and 0.

Outcomes and Valences:

An outcome is anything that might possibly result from performance. High-level performance conceivably might produce a pay raise, a promotion, recognition from the boss, fatigue, stress, and less time to rest. The valence of an outcome is the attractiveness or unattractiveness of that outcome to the person. Pay raises, promotions, and recognition might all have positive valences, whereas fatigue, stress, and less time to rest might all have negative valences. People vary in the strength of their outcome valences. Stress may be a significant negative factor for one person but only a slight annoyance for another. Similarly, a pay increase may have a strong positive valence for someone desperately in need of money, a slight positive valence for someone interested mostly in getting a promotion, and even a negative valence for someone in an unfavorable tax position.

The basic expectancy framework suggests that three conditions must be met before motivated behaviour will occur. First, the effort-to-performance expectancy must be well above zero. The individual must have a reasonable expectation that an exertion of effort will produce high levels of performance. Second, the performance-to-outcome expectancies also must be well above zero. The person must believe that performance may realistically result in valued outcomes. Third, the sum of all the valences for the potential outcomes relevant to the person must be positive. One or more valences may be negative so long as the positives outweigh the negatives. For example, stress and fatigue may have moderately negative valences, but *if* pay, promotion, and recognition have very high positive valences, the overall valence of the set of outcomes associated with performance will still be positive. Conceptually, the valences of all relevant outcomes and the correspondence pattern of expectancies are assumed to interact in an almost mathematical fashion" determine the level of motivation. Most people do assess likehoods of and, references for various consequences of behaviour, but they seldom approach them. In a sense, this is a modern expression of what Martin Luther observed centuries ago when he said, " Every thing that is done in the world is done in hope".

In greater detail, Vroom's theory is that people's motivation toward doing anything will be determined by the value they place on the outcome of their effort (whether positive or negative), multiplied by the confidence they have that their efforts will materially aid in achieving a goal. In other words, Vroom makes the point that motivation is a product of the anticipated worth that an individual places on a goal and the chances he or she sees of achieving that goal. Using his own terms, Vroom's theory may be stated as:

Force = Valence x Expectancy

where force is the strength of a person's motivation, Valence is the strength of an individual's preference for an outcome, and Expectancy is the probability that a particular action will lead to a desired outcome. When a person is indifferent about achieving a certain goal, a valence of zero occurs; there is a negative valence when the person would rather not achieve the goal. The result of either would be, of course, no motivation. Likewise, a person would have no motivation to achieve a goal if the expectancy were zero or negative. The force exerted to do something will depend on both valence and expectancy. Moreover, a motive to accomplish some action might be determined by a desire to accomplish something else. For example, a person might be willing to work hard to get out a product for a valence in the form of pay or a manager might be willing to work hard to achieve company goals in marketing or production for a promotion or pay valence.

Evaluation of Expectancy Theory

Expectancy theory has repeatedly been tested by organizational behaviour researchers. As noted earlier, the complexity of the theory has been both a blessing and a curse. Nowhere is this double-edged quality more apparent than in the research undertaken to evaluate the theory.

Several studies have supported various parts of the theory. Both kinds of expectancy and valence have been found to be associated with effort and performance. Research has also confirmed expectancy theory's claims that people will not engage in motivated behaviour unless they (1) value the expected rewards, (2) believe their efforts will lead to performance, and (3) believe their performance will result in the desired rewards.

However, expectancy theory is so complicated that researchers have found it quite difficult to *test*. In particular, the measures of various parts of the model may lack validity; and the procedures for investigating relationships among the variables. Often have been less scientific than researchers would like. Moreover, people are seldom as rational and objective in choosing behaviours as expectancy theory implies. Still the logic of the model, combined with the consistent, albeit modest, research support for it, suggests that the theory has much to offer.

Managerial Implications of Expectancy Theory

Because expectancy theory is so complex, it is difficult to apply directly in the workplace. A manager would need to figure out what rewards each employee wants and how valuable those rewards are to each individual, measure the various expectancies, and finally adjust the relationships to create motivation. Nevertheless, expectancy theory offers several important and relevant guidelines for the practicing manager. Nadler and Lawler recently summarized these guidelines:

--Determine the primary outcomes each employee wants.

--Decide what levels and kinds of performance are needed to meet organizational goals.

--Make sure the desired levels of performance are possible.

--Link desired outcomes and desired performance.

--Analyze the situation for conflicting expectancies.

--Make sure the rewards are large enough.

--Make sure the overall system is equitable for everyone.

The Vroom Theory and Practice

Once of the great attractions of the Vroom theory is that it recognizes the importance of various individual needs and motivations. It thus avoids some of the simplistic features of the Maslow and Herzberg approaches. It does seem more realistic. It fits the concept of harmony of objectives. Individuals have personal goals different from organizational goals, but these can be harmonized. Furthermore, Vroom's theory is completely consistent with the system of managing by objectives.

The strength of Vroom's theory is also its weakness. His assumption that senses of value vary among individuals at different times and in various places appears to fit real life more accurately. It is consistent also with the idea that a manager's job is to *design* an environment for performance, necessarily taking into account the differences in various situations. On the other hand, Vroom's theory is difficult to apply in practice. Despite its difficulty in application, the logical accuracy of Vrooms theory indicates that motivation is much more complex than the approaches of Maslow and Herzberg seem to imply.

The Porter and Lawler Model

Lyman W. Porter and Edward E. Lawler III derived a substantially more complete model of motivation, built in large part on expectancy theory. In their study, they have applied this model primarily to managers.

As this model indicates, the amount of effort (the strength of motivation and energy exerted) depends on the value of a reward plus the amount of energy a person believes is required and the probability of receiving the reward. The perceived effort and probability of actually getting a reward are, in turn, also influenced by the record of actual performance. Clearly, if people know they can do a job or if they have done it, they have a better appreciation of the effort required and know better the probability of rewards.

Actual performance in a job (the doing of tasks or the meeting of goals) is determined principally by effort expanded. But it is also greatly influenced by an individual's ability (knowledge and skills) to do the job and by his or her perception of what the required task is (the extent to which the person understands the goals, required activities, and other elements of a task); Performance, in turn, is seen as leading to intrinsic rewards (such as a sense of accomplishment or self-actualization) and extrinsic rewards (such as working conditions and status). These rewards, tempered by what the individual sees as equitable, lead to satisfaction. But performance also influences sensed equitable rewards. Understandably, what the individual sees as a fair reward for effort will necessarily affect the satisfaction derived. Likewise, the actual value of rewards will be influenced by satisfaction.

Implications for Practice

The Porter and Lawler model of motivation, while more complex than other theories of motivation, is almost certainly a more adequate portrayal of the system of motivation. To the practicing manager, *this* model means that motivation is not a simple cause and effect matter. It means, too that managers should carefully assess their reward structures and that through careful planning managing by objectives, and clearly defining duties and responsibilities through a good organization structure, the effort performance-reward-satisfaction system can be integrated into an entire system of managing. An important factor in motivation is whether individuals perceive the reward structure as being fair. One way of addressing this issue is through equity theory, which refers to an individual's subjective judgments about the fairness of the reward she or he got, relative to the inputs (which include many factors such as effort, experience, education, and so on), in comparison with the rewards of others. J. Stacy Adams has received a great deal of credit for the formulation of the equity (or inequity) theory. The essential aspects of the equity theory may be shown as follows:

Outcomes by a person	-	*outcomes by another person*
Inputs by a person	-	inputs by another person

There should be a balance of the outcomes-inputs relationship for one person in comparison with that for another person.

If people feel they are inequitably rewarded, they may be dissatisfied, reduce the quantity or quality of output, or leave the organization. They also can ask for a greater reward. If people perceive the rewards as equitable, they probably will continue at the same level of output. If people think the rewards are greater than what is considered equitable, they may work harder. It is also possible that some may discount the reward.

One of the problems is that people may overestimate their own contributions and the rewards others receive. Certain inequities may be tolerated for some time by employees. But prolonged feelings of inequity may result in strong reactions to an apparently minor occurrence. For example, an employee being reprimanded for being a few minutes late may get angry and decide to quit the job, not so much because of the reprimand but because of longstanding feelings that the rewards for his or her contributions are inequitable in comparison with others' rewards. Likewise, a person may be very satisfied with a weekly salary of Rs. 500 until he or she finds out that another person doing similar work gets Rs. 100 more.

REINFORCEMENT THEORY

Psychologist B.F. Skinner of Harvard developed an interesting - but controversial - technique for motivation. This approach, called positive reinforcement or behaviour modification, holds that individuals can be motivated by proper design of their work environment and praise for their performance and that punishment for poor performance produces negative results.

Skinner and his followers do far more than praise good performance. They analyze the work situation to determine what causes workers to act the way they do, and then they initiate changes to eliminate troublesome areas and obstructions to performance. Specific goals are then set with workers' participation and assistance, prompt and regular feedback of results is made available, and performance improvements are rewarded with recognition and praise. Even when performance does not equal goals, ways are found to help people and praise them for the good things they do. It has also been found highly useful and motivating to give people full information on a company's problems, especially those in which they are involved.

This technique sounds almost too simple to work, and many behavioural scientists and managers are skeptical about its effectiveness. However, a number of prominent companies have found the approach beneficial. Air Freight Corporation, for example, observed that this approach saved the company a substantial amount of money by merely inducing employees to take great pains to ensure that containers were properly filled with small packages before shipment.

Perhaps the strength of the Skinner approach is that it is so closely akin to the requirements of good managing. It emphasizes removal of obstructions to performance, careful planning and organizing, control through feedback, and the expansion of communication.

McCLELLAND'S NEEDS THEORY OF MOTIVATION

David C. McClelland has contributed to the understanding of motivation by identifying three types of basic motivating needs. He classified them as the need for power (n/PWR), need for affiliation (n/AFF), and need for achievement (n/ ACH). Considerable research has been done on methods of testing people with respect to these three types of needs, and McClelland and his associates have done substantial research, especially on the need for achievement.

All three drives - power, affiliation, and achievement - are of particular relevance to management, since all must be recognized to make an organized enterprise work well. Because any organized enterprise and every department in' it represents groups of individuals working together to achieve goals, the need for achievement is of paramount importance.

Need for Power

McClelland and other researchers have found that people with a high need for power have a great, concern for exercising influence and control. Such individuals generally are seeking positions of leadership; they are frequently good conversationalists, though often argumentative; they are forceful, outspoken, hardheaded, and demanding; and they enjoy teaching and public speaking.

Need for Affiliation

People with a high need for affiliation usually drive pleasure from being loved and tend to avoid the pain of being rejected by a social group. As individuals, they are likely to be concerned with maintaining pleasant social relationships, to enjoy a sense of intimacy and understanding, to be ready to console and help others in trouble, and to enjoy friendly interaction with others.

Need for Achievement

People with a high need for achievement have an intense desire for success and an equally intense fear of failure. They want to be challenged, and they set moderately difficult (but not impossible) goals for themselves. They take a realistic approach to risk; they are not likely to be gamblers but, rather, prefer to analyze and assess problems, assume personal responsibility for getting a job done, and like specific and prompt feedback on how they are doing. They tend to be restless, like to work long hours, do not worry unduly about failure if it does occur, and tend to like to run their own shows.

Application of 'McClelland's Approach to Managers

In research studies by McClelland and others, entrepreneurs - people who start and develop a business or other enterprise - showed very high need-for achievement and fairly high need-for-power drives but were quite low in their need for affiliation. Managers generally showed high on achievement and power and low on affiliation.

McClelland found the patterns of achievement motivation clearest in people in small companies, with the president normally having very high achievement motivation. In large companies, interestingly enough, he found chief executives to be only average in achievement motivation and often stronger in drives for power and affiliation. Managers in the upper-middle level of management in such companies rated higher than their presidents in achievement motivation. Perhaps, as McClelland indicated, these scores are understandable. The chief executive has "arrived" and those below are striving to advance.

The question is often raised as to whether all managers should rate high on achievement motivation. People who do rate high tend to advance faster than those who do not. But because so much of managing requires other characteristics besides achievement drive, every company should probably have many managers who, while possessing fairly strong achievement motivation, also have a high need for affiliation. This latter need is important for working with people and for coordinating the efforts of individuals working in groups.

Equity Theory of Motivation

First articulated by J. Stacey Adams, equity theory is based on the simple premise that people want to be treated fairly. The theory defines *equity* as the belief that we are being treated fairly in relation to others and *inequity* as the belief that we are being treated unfairly in relation to others.

Equity theory is just one of several theoretical formulations derived from social comparison processes. Social comparisons involve evaluating our own situation in the context of others' situations.

Forming Equity Perceptions

There are four-step process by which people form equity perceptions. Putting this in an organizational setting, the individual first evaluates how she or he is being treated by the organization. Next, the individual develops an evaluation of how a "comparison-other" is being treated. The comparison-other might be a person in the same work group, someone in another part of the organization, or even a composite of several people scattered throughout the organization. After evaluating the treatment of self and other, the individual compares his or her own situation with that of the other. As a consequence of this comparison, the individual tends to perceive either equity or in pending on the strength of this perception, the person may choose to the alternatives.

Adams describes the equity comparison process in terms of input ratios. *Inputs* are an individual's contributions to the organization, education, experience, effort, and loyalty. *Outcomes* are what he or she in return, such as pay, recognition, social relationships, and intrinsic reward. A person's assessment of inputs and outcomes for both self and other are: partly on objective data (for example, the person's own salary) and par perceptions (such as the comparison-other's level of recognition).

The person compares his or her own input-to-outcome ratio with the corresponding ratio of the comparison-other.

A perception of equity does not require that the perceived outcomes and inputs be equal; rather, only their ratios must be the same. A person may believe that his comparison-other deserves to make more money because she works harder; then her higher outcome/input ratio is acceptable. Only if the other's outcomes seem disproportionate to her inputs will the comparison provoke a perception of inequity.

Responses to Perceptions of Equity/Inequity

A perception of equity motivates the person to maintain the status quo. She or he will continue to provide the same level of input to the organization, at least as long as her or his outcomes do not change and the inputs and outcomes of the comparison. other also do not change. A person who perceives inequity, however, is motivated to reduce it: the greater the inequity, the stronger the level of motivation.

Adams has suggested six common methods people use to reduce inequity. First, we may change our own inputs. Thus, a person may put more or less effort into the job, depending on which way the inequity lies, as a way of altering her own ratio. If she believes she is being under rewarded, she may decrease her effort, and vice versa.

Second, we may change our own outcomes. This might include demanding a pay raise, seeking additional avenues for growth and development, or even stealing.

A third, more complex response is to alter our perceptions of ourselves. After perceiving an inequity, for example, a person may change the original self assessment and thus decide that he is really contributing less but receiving more than he originally believed.

The Equity Sensitivity Construct

Equity theory suggests that people want to be treated fairly. It goes on to suggest that individuals base their assessments of equity on comparisons of their inputs and outcomes relative to those of others. The theory also proposes that people will be motivated to reduce or eliminate perceptions of inequity.

Professors Richard C. Huseman and John D. Hatfield of the University of Georgia and Professor Edward W. Miles of Georgia State University recently developed a concept they call equity sensitivity. They suggest that not everyone will respond to perceptions of equity or inequity with the same level of intensity. Instead, responses will be influenced by the individual's preferences for different outcome/input ratios.

Their research findings have led them to suggest three equity sensitivity types. First are the "Benevolents", those who are inclined to work hard for relatively less money. In other words, they are willing to give a lot to their organizations and will be less sensitive to any minor inequities that exist.

The second type, "Entitled", are just the opposite. Entitled believe the organization owes them a great deal and they should not have to do much in return. Thus, for them to experience equity, things really must be inequitable in their favour.

Finally, "Equity Sensitive" most typically fit the equity theory model; that is, they generally experience equity or inequity in accordance with the basic predictions of the theory. More research is needed to help us fully understand equity sensitivity. However, it makes intuitive sense and has received tentative support from preliminary studies. Research evidence provides stronger support for responses to underpayment than for responses to overpayment, but overall, most studies appear to uphold the basic premises of the theory. One interesting new twist on equity theory, explored more fully in *A Look at the Research,* suggests that some people are more sensitive than others to perceptions of inequity.

Managerial Implications of Equity Theory

For managers, the most important implication of equity theory relates to organizational rewards and reward systems. Because "formal" organizational rewards (pay, task assignments) are more easily observable than "informal" rewards (intrinsic satisfaction, feelings of accomplishment), they often are at the center of a person's equity perceptions. Social comparisons clearly are a powerful factor in the workplace.

Equity theory offers managers three messages. First, everyone in the organization needs to understand the basis for rewards. If people are to be rewarded more for high-quality work than for quantity of work, that fact needs to be clearly communicated to everyone. Second, people tend to take a multifaceted view of their rewards; they perceive and experience a variety of rewards, some tangible and others intangible. Finally, people base their actions on their perceptions of reality. If two people make exactly the same salary but each thinks the other makes more, each will base his or her experience of equity on the perception rather than on reality. Hence, even if a manager believes two employees are being fairly rewarded, the employees themselves may not necessarily agree them in such a calculating manner. *The Ethical Dilemma* describes one interesting-and significant-exception.

The Porter-Lawler Extension

Vroom's original presentation of expectancy theory placed it in the mainstream of contemporary motivation theory. Since then, the model has been refined and extended. Most modifications have focused on the identification and measurement of outcomes and expectancies. An exception is the version of expectancy theory presented by Lyman W. Porter and Edward E. Lawler, which takes a novel view of the relationship between employee satisfaction and

THEORIES OF MOTIVATION

Theory	Individual	Summary
Hierarchy of Needs	Abraham Maslow	Five needs rank in anhierarchical order from lowest to highest: physiological, safety, belonging esteem, and self-actualization. An individual moves up the hierarchy and when a need is substantially realized, moves up to the next needs.
Theory X-Theory Y	Douglas McGregor	Proposes two alternative sets of assumption that managers hold about human beings : Motivations-One, basically negative, labeled Theory X; and the other, basically positive, labeled Theory Y. McGregor argues that the Y assumptions are more valid than Theory X and that employee motivation would be maximized by giving workers greater job involvement and autonomy.
Motivation Hygine	Frederick Herzberg	Argues that intrinsic job factors motivate, whereas extrinsic factors only placate employees.
Achievement, Affiliation and Power Motives	David McClelland	Proposes that there are three major needs in workplace situations: achievement, affiliation, and power. A high need to achieve has been positively related to higher work performance when jobs provide responsibility, feedback, and moderate challenge.
Equity Theory	J. Stacey Adams	An individual compares his or her input/outcome his or her input/outcome ratio to relevant others. If there is a perceived inequity, the individual will augment his or her behaviour, or choose another comparison referent.
Expectancy Theory	Victor Vroom	Proposes that motivation is a function of valence (value) of the effort - performance and the performance - reward relationships.

performance. Although the conventional wisdom was that satisfaction leads to performance, Porter and Lawler argued the reverse: If rewards are adequate, high levels of performance may lead to satisfaction.

A MODEL OF MOTIVATION :

The motivation process is complex. Because individuals, and organizations for that matter, are multifaceted, there must exist an appropriate blend of factors that promote needs satisfaction. Furthermore, the factors that must exist may also change frequently-what one has as an unfulfilled need today may not be important tomorrow. Research has shown us that people do change over time; that at various stages in their careers, certain goals are more important than others. For example, consider just two possible "outcomes"-a three-day weekend for the summer months, or a Rs. 4,000 annual bonus. That is what Tina Irwin of Friendship Cards posed to her employees. Tina believed that all her employees would value a Rs. 4,000 bonus; most of them were under 30 years of age, and she thought that an infusion of that kind of money almost 10 percent of their salary-would be welcomed. But Tina was mistaken: When she asked her employees what they valued more, the majority asked for the threeday weekend.

Although another group of employees might have responded differently, there's an important message here: That is, to be sure that specific needs are satisfied, you might have to ask employees what are those needs. Even the best motivational device is useless if it misses its intended target. HRM must ensure that all the potential traps that can sap an individual's motivation are removed. To begin, HRM must ensure that employees clearly see a strong relationship between effort and performance.

The Effort - Performance Relationship

Whenever we hire an employee, there is an implied understanding that we have hired the individual who best fits the job requirements. Accordingly, one of the initial components of the effort-performance relationship focuses on one's ability to exert the appropriate effort. We said earlier that effort is an inward reaction that is witnessed as outward behaviour. But what should that effort be? For motivation to occur, we must be able to specify what effort is needed. For HRM, this means that jobs must be analyzed properly (and updated frequently) to ensure that the job is defined in terms of the tasks, duties, and responsibilities. Furthermore, HRM must identify what the job incumbent must possess to be successful. Once these two concepts are in place, HRM must ensure that it has selected the appropriate person for the job adapted them to the organization and trained them in doing the job the company way. In fact, the effort component is indeed the first two legs of our HRM model-staffing, and training and development. By defining the job properly and selecting the appropriate person, we have those competent, adapted individuals with up-to-date skills, knowledge, and abilities. For job performance purposes, staffing and training and development functions serve to address the "ability" component.

In addition to ability, effort also implies job design. In doing so, a company must assure that employees have the best equipment available to do the job. Even the best ability on a paper-oriented spreadsheet may not provide the same productivity and quality that a computerized version and laser printer would. Consequently, for effort to be exerted, the right tools must be present. Furthermore, the necessary resources must also be readily available. Consider an individual who must spend a considerable part of each day using specific tools. If the tools are located a distance from the job sight, this individual will be less productive than if the tools were readily accessible.

In as much as ability and job design are critical to effort, so, too, is the performance dimension. All the effort in the world will be lost if it is not directed toward some end. For HRM, that end is performance. Hence, an individual will make the effort as long as there is a good likelihood that he or she will be a successful performer. But what is successful performance? At this stage of the motivation model, performance must be defined. Supervisors must be trained in establishing work standards and communicating these expectations to their employees. These same supervisors must be able to coach their employees and assist them in achieving their performance levels. And for supervisors to be proficient at this, they must be trained by HRM staff in performance-appraisal processes. Only by showing employees that their effort is required for specified performance, and that if such effort exists they will be successful on the job, will the effort-performance linkage be completed. When that milestone has been achieved, it's time to tie this performance to organizational goals.

The Individual Performance - Organizational Goal Relationship

Whenever employees perform their duties, their effort should be guided toward some end. If we have determined the strategic nature of our jobs and linked them accordingly to company objectives, then we can best facilitate their attainment by promoting the appropriate performance. Just as we modified the definition of motivation to include organizational goals, so, too, we need to reveal to employees this critical linkage.

The individual performance-organizational goal relationship is designed to provide something of value to the organization. Just as individuals have unsatisfied needs that cause them to behave in a certain manner, so, too, do organizations. But the organization's unsatisfied needs (unfulfilled goals) cannot be satisfied without the effort of its people. If employees' performance is not adequate to meet company objectives, the company will be less able to "reward" its people. For example, consider General Electric Company, known for decades as an organization with some of the highest paid blue-collar workers in the world, Lincoln Electric's methodology is one in which employees share in company profits. Each year, management and employees determine what goals are to be met. If those goals are achieved, then employees receive a specified amount. Additionally, if the goals are surpassed, as they have been for years, then the employees receive a bonus. How much will they receive? That amount is directly related to the level of worker performance. Accordingly, through a profit-sharing process, the more the employee performance exceeds organizational goals, the greater their share of the profits. In fact, in situations like this, a performance-organizational goal relationship creates a win-win situation for all involved. Even so, caution is in order. Such a linkage does not occur automatically. Rather, it is a function of many parts of the organization, like an extensive performance-appraisal system-being led in part by HRM.

For the performance-organizational goal relationship to function effectively, the organization must set a clear direction. That is, the organization must set its plans for given time periods and communicate those plans downward in the organization, and employees must have control over the performance measures. At each successive level, then, the plans take on more detail, such that at employee levels, each individual knows why his or her job exists and what role it plays in achieving the organization's objectives. At these levels, then, jobs must be clearly focused.

Just as in our first relationship, effort-performance, employees must know what is expected of them. Furthermore, they must know what goal performance is, and how it will be determined.

In most of our organizations, the linkage to successful performance is measured through some performance evaluation instrument. But too often, what we measure, or how we go about the process, may be inappropriate. For example, consider a college professor. Assuming the university has, set its objectives, we recognize that one measurement of these objectives is how much students learned. In one simple way, we might assess this information through student evaluations. Are these evaluations an accurate reflection of the performance organizational goal relationship?

The answer is it depends. Obviously, student reaction is one piece of information. Yet they are not the only thing. What about student testing and other assignments the faculty members evaluate? Aren't they better predictors of what was learned? If learning is the outcome, measured by a quantifiable student evaluation score, can we be certain that a high score is a valid prediction of high learning? Or that a low score indicates the opposite? Suppose one faculty member is viewed as being easy-a high grader, who entertains the class with a variety of stories. If this individual is rated high, was the university's goal met? Quite possibly, no. Conversely, another professor who is rigid in grading, not overly charismatic in the class room, and demands quite a bit of work from students may be rated lower, but has helped students learn more.

Whatever the case may be, we must ensure that performance evaluations operate properly. Doing so requires significant time and effort by managers who evaluate employees.

If all is going as planned, we are getting into a better position to motivate our employees. We have defined our jobs, linked them to the strategic nature of the business, communicated to the employees what they must do to be successful, and then measure the effort properly.

The Organizational Goal-Individual Goal Relationship

Mediatech, a midwesternvideo cassette duplicating company, recognized that something was needed to help its employees feel better about work. Mediatech's management apparently noticed that employees tended to be less productive on Friday afternoons-if, in fact, they were on the job at all. To turn around this situation, the company's management decided to institute a lottery. Each week, the company placed Rs. 250.00 into a lottery drawing, which would be held at the close of business on selected Fridays. Employee pay stubs would then be placed in a drum, with the winner receiving the cash award. The only stipulation was that the employee had to be present to win. Mediatech's game has resulted in better morale, greater productivity, and much better attendance on Fridays.

The point of the Mediatech example is not the lottery drawing; rather, it is that doing something differently excites employees and reinforces attendance. In the past, however, companies generally did not look for unique and creative ways to "turn on" employees; rather, supervisors became complacent about what people really wanted out of their jobs. For years, companies held that rewarding employees meant giving pay raises and some recognition here and there. If each of us has specific unsatisfied needs that cause us to behave in a particular manner, how can we be expected to meet all those different needs with one reward system? We can't, generally. Rather, we must tailor our rewards to meet those individual needs, if for no other reason than that such a diverse work force exists, one that indicates various needs must be met. That is' the thrust of this last linkage. The organization requires specific activities to be met to accomplish its goals; why should employees be any different? Hence, if we truly want to enhance motivation, we must make sure individual goals are met.

This can be done through careful assessment of employee needs and a reward system that reflects individual preferences. It's working in companies like Levi-where satisfied employees don't quit, and they remain productive.

If you were to poll every member of your class, you might find that each has a different reason for being there. Some attend because they want to learn more about the subject; some go because it is required, or they fear that missing classes will result in poorer test scores and a lower grade. Some may even be there out of habit-they go to class because that's what they think they're supposed to do. Whatever the reason, each student has a compelling drive that brings him or her to class. Therefore, to satisfy each class member, the instructor must address these diverse needs. But professors will not know what these needs are unless they ask. Ever wonder why some classes start by asking you for your expectations of the course? The instructor is gathering information on your specific needs so that throughout the semester, they can be met. In cases where a student's expectations go outside the intended class syllabus, the instructor knows that additional materials or reading lists may be needed to fulfill that student's expectations. Unfortunately, not all businesses have entirely gotten to this point. There are cases at companies, where individual rewards are tailored to meet specific individual needs. In such companies, this is done through a process called flexible compensation. Let's look at how this works.

In organizations, there's been a tendency to provide uniform benefits. Everyone, for instance, may get medical coverage and reimbursement for night courses taken at the local college. But flexible compensation programs allow people to choose the mix that best fits their needs. Suppose, for example, an individual values more time off from work rather than a bonus or other benefits. Where this freedom to choose does exist, individual choices can be handled. In such companies, employees are presented with a pool of money that reflects increases due to achieving organizational goals through successful performance. Each employee is also presented with a menu of what options are available for the next year and how much each will cost. Employees can choose the benefits they want until they've spent their budgeted amount. Someone wanting more health or life insurance coverage might choose that over more pension contribution, more time off, or extended day care-the employer can purchase those things that are best-suited to his or her individual needs.

Flexible compensation, then, gives choices and allows employees to tailor benefits to their unique needs. Although flexible compensation systems can be expensive to implement and administer, where they exist the benefits have outweighed the costs.

In addition to formulating compensation programs, companies also need to review how their reward and recognition programs operate. For example, suppose the local McDonald's hamburger outlet puts the "employee of the month's" name on a sign beside the counter. Not everyone places a high value on such recognition. Doing something that employees see as low in value does not create the desired effect on motivation we want. Consequently, we may want to recognize superior performance by giving employees a choice and letting them select the reward they most value. Maybe an employee would like dinner for herself and her spouse, or a night at a downtown luxury hotel. Or maybe an employee wants to pick out something from a catalog that he has wanted for a long time. Our point is that the same amount of money spent on a plaque might be better spent letting employees select their rewards.

HRM, then, must ensure that processes are in place that result in employees getting something they want. Yet above all, these rewards must be perceived as being directly attributable to their performance. Only by creating and supporting the performance-reward link will both the employee be motivated and rewarded and the organization be more productive and moving toward meeting its goals.

Putting the Pieces Together

The model we have presented has a number of implications. For one, it shows the need for sound inception and development efforts on the part of HRM. It also reveals that pay-for-performance can be beneficial to both employee and company. Until we begin to reinforce that productivity and show that only productivity matters, we will continue to get things other than the productivity that we reward.

Yet there is another point of the model that is interesting: The motivation process can be adapted to reflect corporate values of what is important for both the organization and the employee.

Implications of the model for motivating employers:

Organizations, today are recognizing the importance of having a highly energized work force. To bring this about, they're using more self-managed work teams, allowing for more worker participation, and empowering their employees. But it is still a long way from being ingrained into the everyday life of most companies.

For example, it has been suggested that supervisors, for whatever reasons, are not providing accurate feedback to individuals about their performance. These supervisors find that identifying group-task goals and linking them to task responsibilities of individual members is a time-consuming operation. Mutual goal setting (the sharing of the goal-setting task with the employee) is avoided by some supervisors because they believe this is an infringement of management prerogatives. In some cases, task goals are identified, performance is evaluated, and the results are conveyed to the employee; yet the employee remains unsure of management's view of his or her accomplishments in terms of reestablished goals. In summary, it appears that many supervisors fail to recognize the importance of establishing goals and performance feedback as would be suggested by the model.

Furthermore, the model suggests that supervisors should ensure that high productivity and good work performance lead to the achievement of personal goals. Again, a review of actual organizational practices reveals many exceptions. Unfortunately, organizations too often fail to allocate rewards in such a way as to optimize motivation. While individual performances tend to be widely divergent-that is, a few outstanding, a few very poor, and the majority' surrounding the average-rewards tend to be allocated more uniformly. The result is the over-rewarding of incompetence and the under-rewarding of superior performance. Employees perceive that hard work does not necessarily payoff; they place a low probability on its leading to organizational rewards, and eventually the attainment of personal goals.

Internal politics is also a vital determinant of who and what will be rewarded. For example, group acceptance may be a personal goal, and high productivity may hinder rather than support achievement of this goal-that is, if the work group one has joined works at a slower pace, leaves exactly at the end of their shift, and takes their breaks precisely on schedule (irrespective of the work that may need to get done at that moment), one must exhibit those same work behaviours to become "part of the gang." Although, at times, these are the realities of work behaviour, our motivational theories tend to overemphasize the decision-making, goal-oriented rationality of human beings. For example, when unemployment is high, there may be a tendency for work groups to work at a place that helps keep their jobs.

While the preceding discussion presents a rather pessimistic view, we offer some suggestions to help motivate employees. These suggestions focus on getting tomorrow's supervisors to understand their employees as individuals, rather than trying to judge them based on their own value system. Again, with a diverse work group, it is unlikely that any supervisor's employees will share all of his or her values.

1. *Address Individual difference* : Recognize that employees are not homogeneous. Rather, each individual possesses a unique set of needs. Accordingly, to effectively motivate any individual, you must understand what those needs are that make them provide the effort.

2. *Properly place employees* : Employees should be properly matched to the job. The best intention will do little for productive behaviour if the employee lacks the ability to get the job done. Proper recruiting and selection techniques should assist in creating this match.

3. *Set achievable goals* : Employees ofter work best when challenging, but achievable goals are matually set. These hard and specific goals provide the direction employees may need. Continuous feedback on how well employees are performing helps to reinforce their effort.

4. *Individualize reward* : Realizing that employees have different needs should indicate that reward, too, may need

to be different. What works for one individual may not "motive" another. As such, one should use their understanding of employee differences and tailor rewards to meet these various needs.

5. *Reward performance* : Rewarding individuals for anything other than performance only reinforces that performance may not matter most. Each reward (individual rewards) must be shown to be the result of achieving organizational goals.

6. *Use an equitable system* : The rewards individuals receive should be viewed as comparable to the effort they have expended. Although perceptions may vary in what is equitable, effort must be made to ensure the reward system used is fair, consistent, and objective.

JOB DESIGNS TO INCREASE MOTIVATION

The Job Characteristics Model

If the type of work a person does is important, we can identify those specific job characteristics that affect productivity, motivation, and satisfaction. A model has been developed by J Richard Hackman and Greg R. Oldham that identifies five such job factors and their interrelationship. It is called the **Job characteristics model.** The research with this model indicates that it can be a useful guide in redesigning the jobs of individuals.

The model specifies five core characteristics or dimensions:

1. *Skill variety-* the degree to which a job requires a variety of different activities so one can use a number of different skills and talents.

2. *Task identity-*the degree to which the job requires completion of a whole and identifiable piece of work.

3. *Task significance-*the degree to which the job has a substantial impact on the lives or work of other people.

4. *Autonomy*-the degree to which the job provides substantial freedom, independence, and discretion to the individual in scheduling the work and in determining the procedures to be used in carrying it out.

5. *Feedback*-the degree to which carrying out the work activities required by the job results in the individual obtaining direct and clear information about the effectiveness of his or her performance.

Individuals with a high growth need are more likely than their low-growth-need counterparts to experience the critical psychological states when their jobs are enriched, and to respond more positively to the psychological states when they are present.

An example of how 'this model works can be seen at J.K. Steel. The industry has had severe problems in the past few decades, but J.K. Steel has become one of the world's lowest-cost producers. To achieve that distinction, the company began to change the jobs of the employees. Employees were trained to do a variety of jobs that increased task variety, task identity, and task significance. In fact, employees were given the opportunities to redesign production-process machinery to make life easier for them, and to cut costs for the organization employees are given a lot of freedom to complete their jobs (autonomy) and are recognized by management for a job well done (feedback).

The core job dimensions can be analyzed and combined into a single index called the motivating potential score (MPS). Jobs that are high on motivating potential--as derived by answers to specific questions for each dimension--must be high on at least one of the three factors that lead to experiencing meaningfulness, and they must be high on both autonomy and feedback. If jobs score high on motivating potential, the model predicts that motivation, performance, and satisfaction will be positively affected, while the likelihood of absence and turnover is lessened.

Research findings on the job characteristics model have been generally supportive. These studies have shown that:

1. People who work on jobs with high-core job dimensions are more motivated, satisfied, and productive than those who do not.

2. People with strong growth needs respond more positively to jobs that are high in motivating potential than do those with weak growth dimensions.

3. Job dimensions operate through the psychological states in influencing personal and work outcome variables, rather than influencing them directly.

These findings support a position that the structure of work is an important influence on an employee's motivation level. Certainly the decision about how a job is to be structured reflects other considerations (such as technology, the environment, plant and equipment, and skill levels) besides its motivational potential. But the design of a job and the way work is scheduled are variables that (1) management can readily influence, and (2) affect an employee's motivation.

Job Enrichment

The most popularly advocated structural technique for increasing an employee's motivational potential is job enrichment. To enrich a job, management allows the worker to assume some of the tasks executed by his or her supervisor. Enrichment requires that workers do increased planning and controlling of their work, usually with less supervision and more self-evaluation. From the standpoint of increasing the internal motivation from doing a job, it has been proposed that job enrichment offers great potential. However, job enrichment is successful only when it increases responsibility, increases the employee's freedom and independence, organizes tasks so as to allow individuals to do a complete activity, and provides feedback to allow individuals to correct their own performance. These aspects are precisely what the job characteristics model advocates. In addition, we can say that these factors lead, in part, to a better quality of work life (QWL). Furthermore, job-enrichment efforts will only be successful if the individuals in the enriched jobs find that their needs are met by the "enrichment". If these individuals did not want increased responsibility, for example, then increasing responsibility will not have the desired effect. Successful job enrichment, then, is contingent on worker input.

A successful job enrichment program should ideally increase employee satisfaction and commitment. But since organizations do not exist to create employee satisfaction as an end, there must also be direct benefits to the organization. There is evidence that job enrichment and QWL programs produce lower absenteeism, reduce turnover costs, and increase employee commitment, but on the critical issue of productivity, the evidence is inconclusive, or poorly measured. In some situations, job enrichment has increased productivity; in others, productivity has been decreased. However, when it decreases, there does appear to be a consistently conscientious use of resources and a higher quality of product or service. In other words, in terms of efficiency, for the same input a higher quality of output is obtained; so fewer repairs could increase productivity if the measure included the number of repairs.

Motivating a Diverse Work Force

Studies tell us that men place considerably more importance on having autonomy in their jobs than do women. In contrast, the opportunity to learn, convenient work hours, and good interpersonal relations are more important to women than to men. HRM needs to recognize that what motivates a single mother with two dependent children who's working full time to support her family may be very different from the needs of a young, single, part-time worker or the older employee who is working to supplement his or her pension income. Employees have different personal needs and goals that they're hoping to satisfy through their job. Offering various types of rewards to meet these diverse needs can be highly motivating for employees. We've seen some of these before. For instance, family-friendly benefits and flexible work schedules are a response to the varied needs of a diverse work force.

Motivating a diverse work force also means that HRM policies must be flexible by being considerate of cultural differences. The theories of motivation we refer were developed largely by U.S. psychologists and validated by studying American workers. Therefore, these theories need to be modified for different cultures.

For instance, the self-interest concept is consistent with capitalism and the extremely high value placed on individualism in countries such as the United States.

Results, however, of several recent studies among employees in countries other than the United States indicate that some aspects of the motivation process are transferable. For instance, the motivation process was presented as a means of changing performance-related behaviours. However, we shouldn't assume that motivation concepts are universally applicable. HRM must adjust its motivational techniques to fit the societal culture. For example, the method of recognizing and embarrassing the worst sales clerks by giving them awards used by a large department store in Xian, China may be effective in China. But doing something that humiliates employees isn't likely to work in India.

Pay for Performance

Our knowledge of motivation tells us that people do what they do to satisfy some need. Before they do anything, therefore, they look for a payoff or reward. Although there may be many different rewards offered by organizations, most of us are concerned with earning an amount of money that allows us to satisfy our needs and wants. Because pay is an important variable in motivation as one type of reward, we need to look at how we can use pay to motivate high levels of employee performance. And this explains the intent and logic behind pay-for-performance programs.

Pay-for-performance programs are compensation plans that pay employees on the basis of some performance measure. Piece-rate plans, gainsharing, wage-incentive plans, profit sharing, and lump sum bonuses are examples of pay-for-performance programs. What differentiates these forms of pay from the more traditional compensation plans is that instead of paying an employee for time on the job, pay is adjusted some performance measures. These performance measures might include such things as individual productivity, team or work group productivity, departmental productivity, or the overall organization's profits for a given period.

Performance-based compensation is probably most compatible with the process of motivation. That is, employees should perceive a strong relationship between their performance and the rewards they receive if motivation is to be maximized. If rewards are allocated solely on nonperformance factors--such as seniority, job title, or across the board cost-of-living raises then employees are likely to reduce their efforts.

Pay-for-performance programs are gaining in popularity in organizations. One survey of 2000 companies found that almost 70 percent of firms surveyed were practicing some on of pay-for-performance for salaried employees. The growing popularity can be explained in terms of a motivation tool. From a motivation perspective, making some or all of a worker's pay conditional on performance measures focuses his or her attention and effort on that measure, then reinforces the continuation of that effort with rewards. However, if the employee, team, or the organization's performance declines, so too does the reward. Thus, there's an incentive to keep efforts and motivation strong.

A recent extension of the pay-for-performance concept is called competency-based compensation. A competency-based compensation program pays and rewards employees based on the skills, knowledge, or behaviours employees' possess. These competencies may include such behaviours and skills as leadership, problem solving, decision making, or strategic planning. Based on the degree to which these competencies exist, pay levels are established. Pay increases in a competency based system are awarded for growth in personal competencies, as well as the contributions one makes to the overall organization. Accordingly, an employee's rewards are tied directly to how capable he or she is to contributing ,to the success of the organization's goals and objectives.

Motivating through Employee Stock Ownership Plans

Many companies are using employee stock ownership plans for improving and motivating employee performance. An employee stock ownership plan (ESOP) is a compensation program in which employees become part owners of the organization by receiving stock as a performance incentive. More than 10 million employees in such companies as United Airlines, British Petroleum, Avis, NationsBank, Pfizer, Thrifty Foods, Owens Coming, Weirton Steel, and Starbucks participate in ESOPS. Also, many ESOPs allow employees to purchase additional stocks at attractive, below-market prices. Under an ESOP, employees often are motivated to give more effort because it makes them owners who will share in any gains and losses. The fruits of their labours are no longer just going into the pockets of some unknown owners-the employees are the owners.

The research on ESOPs indicates that they increase employee satisfaction and frequently result in higher performance. For instance, one study compared 45 ESOP companies against 238 companies that did not have ESOPs. The ESOP firms outperformed the non-ESOP organizations in terms of both employment and sales growth. However, other studies showed that productivity in organizations with ESOPs does increase but the impact is greater the longer the ESOP has been in existence. So organizations shouldn't expect immediate increases in employee motivation and productivity if an ESOP is implemented. But over time, employee productivity and satisfaction should go up. Other studies also show that ESOPs work better in smaller, private firms where "worker-input issues are easier to handle."

Although ESOPs have the potential to increase employee satisfaction and work motivation, employees need to psychologically experience ownership in order to realize this potential. This means that in addition to merely having a financial stake in the organization, employees need to be regularly informed on the status of the business to have the opportunity to exercise influence over the operation. When these conditions are met, "employees will be more satisfied with their jobs, more satisfied with their organizational identification, motivated to come to work, and motivated to perform well while at work.

Motivating Minimum Wage Employees

Imagine for a moment that your first supervisory job after graduating from college involves overseeing a group comprised of minimum wage employees. Offering more pay to these employees for high levels of performance is out of the question. Your company just can't afford it. What are your motivational options at this point? One of the toughest motivation challenges facing HRM is how to achieve high performance levels among minimum wage workers.

One trap many in HRM fall into is thinking that employees are only motivated by money. And although money is important as a motivator, it's not the only "reward" that people seek and that one can use. In motivating minimum wage employees, HRM should look at other types of rewards that serve the function of helping motivate employee performance.

Some other types of rewards can be also used. Many companies use employee recognition programs such as employee of the month, quarterly employee-performance award ceremonies, or other celebrations of employee accomplishment. Such programs serve the purpose of highlighting employees whose work performance has been of the type and level the organization wants to encourage. We must educate supervisors on the power of praise. When used, we must ensure that these "pats on the back" are sincere and done for the right reasons; otherwise, employees can see such actions as manipulative.

But we know from the motivation process previously presented that rewards are only part of the motivation equation. We can look to job design, too, for additional insights. In service industries such as travel and hospitality, retail sales, child care, and maintenance, where pay for front-line employees generally doesn't get much above the minimum wage level, successful companies are empowering these front-line employees with more authority to address customers' problems. If we use them to examine this change, we can see that this type of job redesign provides enhanced motivating potential because employees now experience increased skill variety, task identity, task significance, autonomy, and feedback.

REFERENCES

Richard A. Cosier and Dan R. Dalton, "Equity Theory and Time: A Reformulation", *Academy of Management Review,* April 1983, pp. 311-319.

See Jerald Greenberg, "Cognitive Reevaluation of Outcomes in Response to Underpayment Inequity", *Academy of Management Journal,* March 1989, pp. 174-184.

Edward C. Tolman, *Purposive Behavior in Animals* (New York: Appleton-Century-Crofts, 1932); Kurt Lewin, *The Conceptual Representation and the Measurement of Psychological Forces* (Durham, N.c.: Duke University Press, 1938).

Victor Vroom, *Work and Motivation* (New York: Wiley, 1964).

See Carlla S. Smith and Michael T. Brannick, "A Role and Expectancy Model of Participative Decision-Making: A Replication and Theoretical Extension", *Journal of Organizational Behavior,* March 1990, pp. 91-104.

Lyman W. Porter and Edward E. Lawler, *Managerial Attitudes and Performance* (Homewood, Ill.: Dorsey Press, 1968).

David A. Nadler and Edward E. Lawler, "Motivation: A Diagnostic Approach," in J. Richard Hackman, Edward E. Lawler, and Lyman W. Porter, eds., *Perspectives on Behavior in Organizations,* 2nd ed. (New York: McGraw-Hill, 1983), pp. 67-78.

Terence R. Mitchell, "Expectancy Models of Job Satisfaction, Occupational Preference, and effort: A Theoretical, Methodological, and Empirical Appraisal", *Psychological Bulletin,* vol. 81, 1974, pp. 1096-1112;

John P. Campbell and Robert D. Pritchard, "Motivation Theory in Industrial and Organizational Psychology", in Marvin D. Dunnette, ed., *Handbook of Industrial and Organizational Psychology* (Chicago: Rand McNally, 1976), pp. 63-130.

Wanous, Keon, and Latack, "Expectancy Theory and Occupational/Organizational Choices", Pinder, *Work Motivation.*

Pinder, *Work Motivation.*

Campell and Pritchard, "Motivation Theory in Industrial and Organizational Psychology"). Pinder, *Work Motivation.*

John P. Campbell, Marvin D. Dunnette, Edward E. Lawler, and Karl E. Weick, *Managerial Behavior, Performance, and Effectiveness* (New York: McGraw-Hill, 1970).

J. Stacey Adams, "Toward an Understanding of Inequity", *Journal of Abnormal and Social Psychology,* November 1963, pp. 422-436. See also Richard T. Mowday",Equity Theory Predictions of Behavior in Organizations", in Richard M. Steers and Lyman W. Porter; eds., *Motivation and Work Behavior,* 4th ed. (New York: McGraw-Hill, 1987), pp. 89-110, and Richard C. Huseman, John D. Hatfield, and Edward W. Miles, "A New Perspective on Equity Theory: The Equity Sensitivity Construct", *Academy of Management Review,* October 1987, pp. 222-234.

Paul S. Goodman, "Social Comparison Processes in Organizations", in Barry M. Staw and Gerald R. Salancik, eds., *New Directions in Organizational Behavior* (Chicago: St. Clair, 1977), pp. 97-131.

J. Stacey Adams, "Inequity in Social Exchange", in L. Berkowitz, ed., *Advances in Experimental Social Psychology,* vol. 2 (New York: Academic Press, 1965), pp. 267-299.

Edward W. Miles. John D. Hatfield, and Richard C. Huseman, "The Equity Sensitivity Construct: Potential Implications for Worker Performance". *Journal of Management,* December 1989, pp. 581-588; Reprinted with permission of Richard C. Huseman. John D. Hatfield, and Edward W. Miles, "A New Perspective on Equity Theory: The Equity Sensitivity Construct", *Academy of Management Review,* April 1987, pp. 222-234.

IV
Raymond Limited
(Textile Div., Chhindwara)
An Overview

"In a world so certain of uncertainties, it is determination and ambition that keeps one going. What shall happen if these qualities are a culture? What can happen, is so for all to see at Raymond limited Chhindwara".

This is the slogan of Raymond Ltd. Chhindwara , which is part of the J K group (Western Zone) situated at a distance of 57 Kms from "Orange city" Nagpur. It is spread over a total area of 100 acres. The 100 acres plot stands as the plant commenced sometimes in July 1990. The plant was in full swing by lst April 1991. In a short span of 3 years, they achieved stupendous success. They have rapidly improved upon the efficiency figures. The Spinning and Weaving departments have charged ahead of 90% efficiency levels. Quite frankly, they have exceeded all expectations.

But then, what are the parameters of performance? Is it PRODUCTION, is it QUALITY, is it the CUSTOMER, or is it the PEOPLE they have? Perhaps, it is an amalgamation of all these that spurs them on.

The present capacity of the plant after expansion, which has been concluded recently, is 25,000 Mtr. of fabric per day. Thus approximately 86 lac Mtr. is produced per annum at Chhindwara. The Finishing Department is the largest of its kind in Asia with a capacity of 40,000 Mtr. per day. This fact opens to the possibility of carrying out finishing for other plants. As of now they process the complete production of JALGAON.

A Wool Washing and a Grey Combing unit have become operational recently which has eliminated their dependency of Thane for scoured wool. Also the capacity of Dyeing Department has been doubled with the commissioning of 11 new HTHP machines. With the commissioning of new P/W spinning the number of spindles have been installed in the new Weaving Department and this has taken the total number of looms to 120. All this makes Raymond Chhindwara the largest producer of P/W fabric among its sister concerns.

Quality of the produce needs no adjective. Quality of final product is a major concern for one and all. Inspection details are followed with religious favour. The minute and craftsmen like corrections in the Mending Section remove whatever faults pass by. An intermediate Perching Section in the Finishing Department is a unique feature. This eliminate minute imperfections after Wet finishing.

The customer's word is THE FINAL VERDICT for the Raymond. The faith the customer has in their product is valued and cherished by all of them. They are suppliers to the novel chain of company retail shops all over the country. There are in total 163 such shops in 75 cities in India.

The HUMAN FORCE here asserts the significance of the glorious capabilities of humanity. Being HUMAN, is what they strive for. Neglecting the employees for harvesting more profit is certainly not their cup of teas. They realise and respect the futility of such an effort.

RAYMOND - CARE

The company has developed a Modern Housing Complex

for their staff. The complex has a Modern Club House with Health Club having facilities like Swimming, Sauna and Gymnasium with latest equipments. The Club House also has an international standard badminton court. They realise the importance of quality education. A school has been started within their housing complex. As of now the school is for up to 12th standard. Children of officers studying in Nagpur can utilise a company Hostel which has all the necessities, a growing child needs. A well equipped Dispensary is maintained in the factory premises. They also have a Baby Creche for children of working mothers.

What is the right input to such an organisation? It is the quality of people. They have selected fresh graduates from campus interviews of reputed colleges. These students are inducted as trainees from a period of one year. The company believes in moulding them in the 'Raymond Culture'. For trainees with no textile background they conduct separate classes (ATA). The company is also towards the completion of a large scale 'General, Awareness Training Programme' for workers in which they will be covering the entire work force.

The future certainly has exciting things in store for them. The 160 crore investment in the expansion project can only take to new heights. With another Denim Project at Yavatmal, just round the corner, the work has just begun.

LOOK FORWARD TO THE CELEBRATION

With satisfied customer of its member companies the J. K. Organisation (Western Division) is today a name to reckon with in India's corporate sector. The J.K. Organisation, of which Raymond (Textile-division Chhindwara) is part, saw the light of the day in 1886. The organisation received its name J.K. from the father son duo of Sh. Juggilal Singhania and Sh. Kamlapat Singhania.

Their idea was to develop an organisation with a diversified product line. Over the years the organisation grew in structure and nature. To facilitate better involvement of the top management in the organisation effort, the J. K. Organisation has been divided into three zones namely Western,Central & Eastern. RAYMOND LIMITED, Chhindwara, is a part of Western zone. The Chairman of this zone is Sh. Vijajpat Singhania, whose zeal to be the best was recently demonstrated when he won the World Lightest Aircraft Race.

RAYMOND becomes a member of the JK group about 60 years back. RAYMOND had been producing blankets as their major product until it decided to change all this, with the introduction of superior quality fabric. Over the last decade or so Raymond has grown a few times from a turnover of Rs 50 crores in 1980s to over 600 crores today. Profits have continually improved with regular and growing dividends. In fact, today, Raymond is a net foreign exchange earner and the real proud is to create a premium brand, which is in international competitive market with other few companies of India.

RAYMOND Ltd. was adjudged the best Indian company and was presented the top corporate award by a team of experts from the HARVARD BUSINESS SCHOOL and THE ECONOMICS TIMES. THE BUSINESS WORLD-MARG survey (1993) placed it at sixth position for overall performance. The group was ranked very high in profitability and innovativeness. According to DALAL STREET JOURNAL the group are at No. 3 at National level and No. 1 in Western India. Undoubtedly they are the Numero Uno in the Indian Textile Industry.

It is not that they were born that. They have achieved this as a result of their burning desire to provide the customer with world class fabrics.

Customer is the most important word in their dictionary. The wide range of shades, designs and blends available in the market bear a testimony to this.

RAYMOND limited is the flagship company of JK Group (Western Division) and has three plants in India, at Thane, Jalgaon and Chhindwara and one in Kenya. The Indian operation has headquarter at Mumbai.

They produce high quality, up market fabric in polyester/wool and polyester/viscose blends. It is not for nothing that they are known as master of shades. They are regularly churning out new shades and designs which help them maintain their market-leader status. The fabric through a final stage of hi-tech processing achieves the now famous RAYMOND'S quality.

The combined operations of Raymond's produced a staggering 160 lacs meters of such hi-quality fabric per year. It is not a matter of coincidence but a result of their quest for excellence that they produced the finest fabric in India, the Microlite and Super Microlite labels. These all wool, extra fine high denier qualities can compare with the best in the world.

The customer's faith in their quality is overwhelming. At the bi-annual top dealer meeting they usually receive orders which are twice the capacity. They plan their produce in approximately six months in advance, since whatever they produce is already sold at the bi-annual meeting. The market calls it fantastic – it is a way of life for them.

They have been appreciated for their innovativeness – why?

It is for one and all to see.

They promoted the Park Avenue brand of ready–made suits and other men's garments and accessories. They are ace supplier for these items produced at JK Bombay. As a matter of habit they have done very well.

Another example of their pioneering efforts is the unique concept of Raymond's Exclusive retail-shops all over the country. There are now 163 such outlets in 75 cities.

A chronological sequence in the life of the factory at Chhindwara may be outlined as follows :

6/4/87 Ministry of Textiles, Government of India issued letter of intent No. LOI 157 (87), at Balaghat, for manufacture of Textiles by installation of 50,000 spindles and 1500 looms (under schedule industry no 23 (5) – synthetic artificial fibres including yarn and not under 23 (3) – wool licensed to Thane and Jalgaon.

28/11/88 MRTP cleared the proposal for setting up a new unit at Boregaon by installation of 50,000 spindles and 1500 looms- total cost of Rs. 335 cores. Synthetic artificial man-made fabric and yarn.

28/11/88 Ministry of Industry (SIA) approved change of location from Balaghat to Boregaon.

30/5/88 LOI was extended up to 5/4/1989.

11/8/89 Raymond signed lease agreement (for 99 yr.) with Madhya Pradesh Kendra Vikas Nigam, Jabalpur, for 100 acres of land at lease premium of Rs. 29,45,283,75 with annual rent growth of Rs. 60,728.

8/10/89 Bhoomi Poojan was performed.

10/10/89 Construction of factory building started.

31/5/90 Raymond signed agreement with MPEB for sanction of HP power up to 1500 KVA after 31/5/90.

up to 3000 KVA after 3/8/90.

up to 5500 KVA after 3/12/90.

20/8/90 South India Viscose Limited dispatched Viscose staple fabric to Boregaon

30/8/90 Indian Organic Chemical Limited diverted a consignment of staple fiber from Orient Synthetic Limited to Raymond and was sent to Bhilwara Spinners, Bhilwara, for converting into yarn.

1/4/91 Commencement of commercial production.

10/6/91 Spinning and Finishing Department started operating.

1/8/91 First sale invoice was raised on Premji Dungarshi Co. Thane, despatched on 25/7/91.

23/2/92 Ministry of Textiles, (Govt. of India) Bombay, allotted registration no TXC/WVG/TTC /28/9/31 dated 22/01/1992 for Boregaon unit.

24/7/93 Districts Industries, Central Chhindwara issued a certificate for exemption of entry tax for a period of 5 yr. from 30/8/90 on entry tax (purchase) in lieu of octroi.

29/5/93 Raymond made an application to Secretariat for industrial approval New Delhi issued Certificate certifying that Raymond started commercial production from 1/4/1991 for production of 15,75,000 Sq. Mtr of all wool fabrics at Boregaon for manufacture for the first time.

15/6/93 Ministry of Industry, Govt. of India, Delhi, issued acknowledgement of the application under the new procedures of licensing for manufacture of woolen fabrics at Boregaon.

4/11/93 Industries Commissioner MP, Bhopal, issued sanctioned order for payment of states investment subsidy of Rs. 15 lakhs for setting of new unit at Boregaon under State Investment Subsidy, Rule 1989.

15/1/94 Director of industries, Govt. of MP, Bhopal, issued certificate of eligibility for exemption of payment of sales tax for a period of 5 yr. from date of commencement of production 1/4/91 to 31/3/96.

24/2/94 Raymond-Boregaon, started commercial production of woolen fabrics.

1/4/94 Provident Fund coverage was given to employees after availing of infancy period of 3 yr. benefit.

14/7/94 Ministry of Industry, Govt. of India, issued acknowledgement for commencement of Commercial Woolen Fabric from 24/1/94.

V

Job Satisfaction of Employees in Raymond Ltd.

Every research is based on certain methodologies without which no research work can be complete. Researcher has adopted a method to carry out the research work, which was found to be suitable. It's a detailed study, based on scientific description. The researcher adopted a procedure and used the following methodology for the study.

Universe of the Study:

The study was limited to Raymond Group at Sausar, in Chhindwara Distt. near Nagpur. The Universe covered the Executives and Labourers of Raymond Ltd. with emphasis on Sausar Unit. The Universe of the study was 330 Labourers and 250 Executives from which samples were selected.

Sampling Procedure:

When the part of the Universe is taken as the representative of the whole, the Study in called Sampling study. There were total 300 employees selected by the researcher using Stratified Random Sampling method. From the randomly selected universe of 330 Labourers and 250 Executives, 300 employees were taken as samples i.e. 150 from each stratum respectively.

The limitation of time and money has not permitted the researcher to study the whole universe. So the researcher studied only 300 employees including both executives and labourers of Raymond Ltd.

Research Design:

Designing is a preliminary step in every activity. It provides a picture for the whole before starting of the work. For this relevant literature related with the subject has been collected. It also includes survey, selection of respondents and proper questioning etc.

It is a descriptive study in which the researcher has tried to access the intensity of Job Satisfaction among Executives and Labourers of Raymond Ltd. by taking a Scientific Scale in consideration. Research was of quantitative method.

Schedule:

The researcher with a view to ensure that complete and uniform data is available devised a schedule containing 50 questions. It was developed in many parts having several questions in each area of concern to the study. These areas were: -

1. General Information.
2. Socio-Economic Background.
3. Working Conditions, Financial Benefits.
4. Promotion Opportunities.
5. Transfer Opportunities.
6. Training Programmes.
7. Welfare Facilities.
8. Inter-personal Relationship.
9. Decision Making.
10. Grievance Redressal and Disciplinary action.
11. Attitude towards Job.

Interview Schedule was pre-tested in a similar population outside the area covered by the study. A final schedule emerged after taking into account the testing experiences. Questions were so arranged as to cause the least possible problem to the respondents in reconstructing the general sequence of events as experienced by them. This meant intermixing of questions from different areas, but every care was taken to include all the areas and relevant questions in each of them in final schedule. The final schedule was structured tool providing for probes and questioning in depth, wherever necessary. After preparing the schedule, 300 copies of the schedule were prepared and distributed. Researcher started the fieldwork and it took 3 months for data collection.

Interview Procedure:

Looking at the nature of study careful consideration was given to interview the employees. The researcher took prior permission and the employees were informed of the purpose of the survey and were assured that information given by them would be treated confidentially.

This study made use of factual statements to introduce the researcher and the study to each employee, the researcher right to ask question was comfortably established. Primary Data collected was then compiled and organised.

Data Processing:

After collecting all the data researcher processed the data. Data processing includes Editing, Coding, Master Chart. It also includes Tabulation and Data Analysis.

a. *Editing*: - First of all the data were edited

b. *Coding*: - Coding implies assigning of symbols to the classified data. Researcher gave system of signs to all the questions and to it multiple answers were given. Interview schedule was assigned different codes for a better understanding.

c. *Tabulations*: - After coding, the information obtained from the interview Schedule was analysed and made in a simple as well as cross table form which were interpreted.

d. *Analysis & Interpretation*: - The information that was obtained from different tables regarding each question was separately analysed and interpreted. Likert (1932) Scale was used by researcher. Responses thus received were given the Scores. Highest the Score most favourable was the attitude.

Strongly Agree	**=**	**5**
Agree	**=**	**4**
Undecided	**=**	**3**
Disagree	**=**	**2**
Strongly Disagree	**=**	**1**

Secondary Data:

Interview with 300 employees was supplemented by consulting relevant literature, Official records, Census records, District Gazetteers. Observation method was utilized to get the data.

Statistical Analysis:

The data was put to further statistical analysis to draw significant conclusions. The data was analysed in terms of percentage, ratios, etc.

Operational Definitions:

Based on the nature and content of study, the following concepts are defined.

1. *Job Satisfaction*: - The term Job Satisfaction refers to an individual's general attitude towards his or her job. It is a pleasurable or positive emotional state resulting from the appraisal of one's job or job experience. There are three important dimensions to job satisfaction. First, job satisfaction is an emotional response to a job situation. Secondly, job satisfaction is often determined by how well one meet or exceed expectations. Third, job satisfaction represents several related attitudes.

2. *Executives*: He is an employee having job of executing and managing the affairs of company. Employees belonging to this grade are from Junior Officer to General Manager.

3. *Labourers*: He is a person employed to do any skilled, Semi-Skilled, Unskilled, Highly Skilled work.

4. *Values*: Values are the basic convictions that a specific mode of conduct is personally or socially preferable or not. They contain a judgemental element of an individual's idea as to what is right, good or desirable.

5. *Attitudes*: Attitudes are evaluative statements either favourable or unfavourable. It is an intention to behave in a certain way towards someone or something.

6. *Scale*: In the present study 5 point Scale (Likert Method, 1932) was used to assess the areas of agreement and disagreement. Few statements positive and negative in nature, which were examined by the Psychologist, were introduced. Responses thus received were given the scores. Highest the score most favourable was the attitude.

In this chapter the researcher has discussed the general socio-economic status of employees of Raymond Ltd. This Chapter also deals with their Value System and certain Job related Attitudes of the employees. The determinants and factors responsible for Job Satisfaction are also analyzed and presented in this chapter. Different areas of Value System, Attitudes and Job Satisfaction are interpreted and reflected through tables in this chapter.

The data analysis of the above-mentioned areas is given in the following pages.

Age:

Age of the respondents is very helpful in determining their way of thinking. Age is one of the factor which accounts for his sense of responsibilities.

Table - 1

Sl. No.	*Age in Years*	*Executives* No.	*Executives* %	*Labourers* No.	*Labourers* %
(a)	21 – 30	30	20	20	13.33
(b)	31 – 40	120	80	80	53.33
(c)	41 – 50	-	-	50	33.34
(d)	51 – 60	-	-	-	-
	Total	**150**	**100**	**150**	**100**

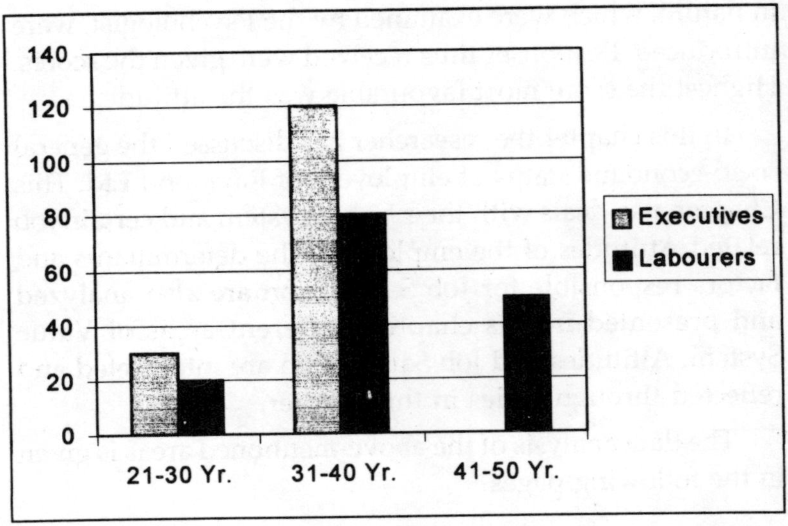

Graph - 1 : Agewise Distribution

The interpretation of the above mentioned table shows that 80 percent of the executives were in the age group of 31 – 40 years, while only 20 percent of the executives fall in the age group of 21 – 30 years.

On the other hand 53.33 percent of the labourers belonged to the age group of 31 - 40 years, while 33.34 percent were in the age group of 41 – 50 years and only 13.33 percent fall in the age group of 21 – 30 years.

The age composition of employees shows that proper manpower planning has been undertaken to ensure smooth operation.

A large chunk of employees i.e. 80 percent of executives and 53.33 percent of labourers were in the age group of 31 – 40 years.

Educational Status: -

Educational status plays a vital role in selecting the right occupation. Educational status is the criteria to place right man on right job.

Table - 2

Sl.No.	*Qualifications*	*Executives*		*Labourers*	
		No.	*%*	*No.*	*%*
(a)	Intermediate	6	4	120	80
(b)	Graduate	54	36	-	-
(c)	Post Graduate	54	36	-	-
(d)	Technical	12	8	30	20
(e)	Professional (M.B.A./B.E.)	24	16	-	-
	Total	**150**	**100**	**150**	**100**

The above table provides the details about the educational qualifications of the executives and labourers of the organization.

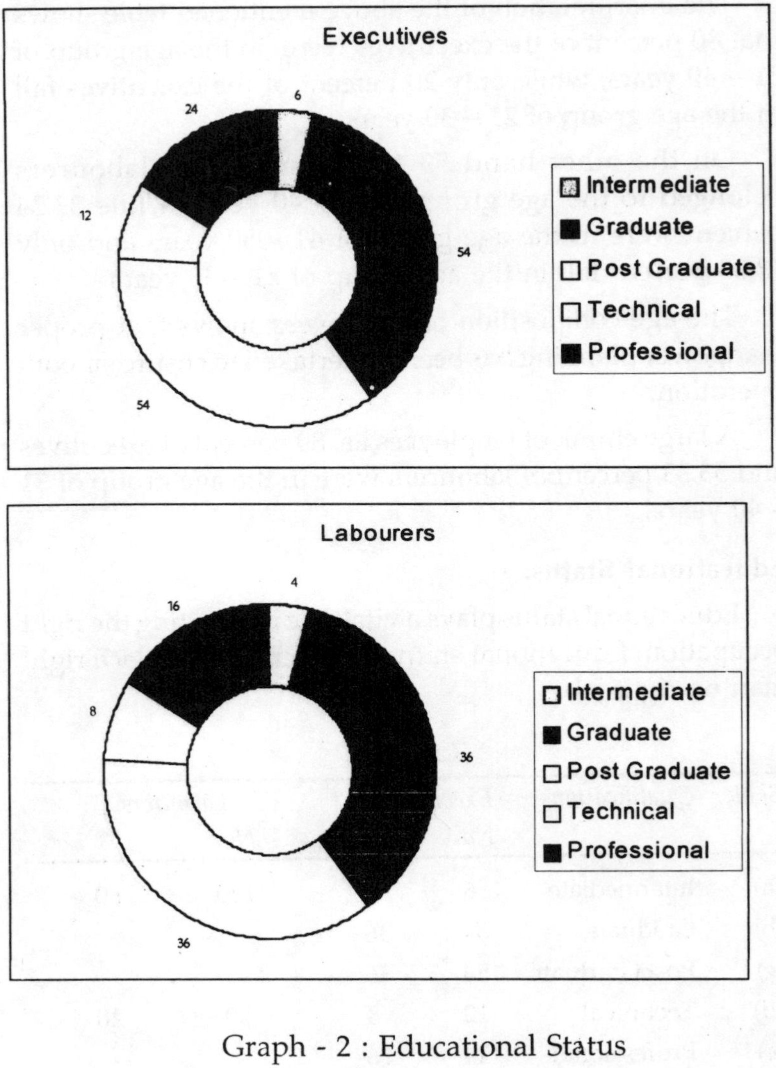

Graph - 2 : Educational Status

On executives side 36 percent were Graduate and Post Graduate respectively, 16 percent of executives were professionally qualified i.e. having M.B.A. B.E. etc., professional degree.

Labourers were mostly intermediate as revealed by 80 percent of them while 20 percent of the labourers were technically qualified i.e., having a Diploma course or ITI etc.

Thus the above table reveals that the executives and labourers were reasonably qualified.

Status of the Job:

Status of the job is indicative of its nature and determines the attitude towards job and willingness to work. Job, which is ad-hoc, may not create right motivation among the employees.

Table - 3

Sl. No.	*Nature of Service*	*Executives*		*Labourers*	
		No.	*%*	*No.*	*%*
(a)	Temporary	-	-	15	10.00
(b)	Contract	-	-	35	23.33
(c)	Permanent	150	100	100	66.67
(d)	Ad-hoc	-	-	-	-
	Total	**150**	**100**	**150**	**100**

It is clear from the above table that all 100 percent of executives were on permanent job, while 66.67 percent of labourers were permanent. The organisation also has contract labour policy, as 23.33 percent belonged to the categories of contract labour. Only 10 percent of the labourers were having temporary nature of job.

Period of Service :

Experience helps a person in doing a job more accurately as its guides in planning his work. It helps him to become more innovative and helps in developing himself.

Table - 4

Sl. No.	*Period of Service*	*No. of Respondents*		*Percentage*	
		No.	%	*No.*	%
(a)	1–4 Yrs.	24	16	18	12.00
(b)	5–9 Yrs.	96	64	40	26.67
(c)	10–14 Yrs.	30	20	92	61.33
(d)	15–19 Yrs.	-	-	-	-
(e)	20–24 & Above	-	-	-	-
	Total	**150**	**100**	**150**	**100**

A glance at the above table makes it clear that 64 percent of executives had worked for 5-14 years, 20 percent of executives for 10-14 years and 16 percent for 1-4 Years. Labourers on the other hand had majority who have worked for 10-14 years as opined by 61.33 percent, while 26.67 percent had worked for 5-9 years and remaining 12 percent of labourers for 1-4 years.

Thus it is clear that both the executives and labourers were experienced enough to deal effectively with their assigned jobs.

Monthly Salary:

Monthly salary is a major factor which may lead to job satisfaction.

Monetary criteria can be a factor of individual satisfaction to fulfill his/her needs or requirements.

Table - 5

Sl. No.	*Monthly Salary*	*Executives*		*Labourers*	
		No.	*%*	*No.*	*%*
(a)	Rs 2000–5000	12	8	122	81.33
(b)	Rs 5001–8000	102	68	28	18.67
(c)	Rs 8001–11000	18	12	-	-
(d)	Rs 11001–14000	18	12	-	-
(e)	Rs 14001& above	-	-	-	-
	Total	**150**	**100**	**150**	**100**

Above table shows the monthly salary of the respondents. Sixty eight percent of the executives were getting a monthly salary ranging between 5001 – 8000. Twelve percent of executives' salary ranged between 8001 – 11000 and 11001 – 14000 respectively. 81.33 percent of labourers were getting salary between 2000 – 5000.

The executives and labourer were getting reasonable monthly salary but this is not the only index of job satisfaction. However, there are various other measures, which altogether add to the job satisfaction.

Living Status:

Residential status shows that basic need of the respondents have been fulfilled. It is also a barometer of individual social and economic status. In the present case many executives and labourers were living in rented accommodation, which shows the policy of administration not to provide housing for all.

Table - 6

Sl. No.	*Living Status*	*Executive*		*Labourers*	
		No.	*%*	*No.*	*%*
(a)	Own House	42	28	24	16
(b)	Factory Accommodation	8	12	6	4
(c)	Rented	90	60	120	80
	Total	**150**	**100**	**150**	**100**

The above table throws a light on the living status of executives and labourers. It can be seen that 60 percent of executives lived an rented houses, and only 12 percent of executives were availing the facility of factory accommodation.

Labourers were also affected by the housing facilities of the organisation. Eighty percent of labourers were residing on rented house, while only 4 percent were enjoying the factory accommodation. It was very strange to know that a prestigious organisation like Raymond Ltd. is unable to provide proper housing facilities for executives as well as labourers. The executives mostly belonged to nearby city of Nagpur and were residing in a town located few kms from the plant. Labourers hailed mostly from the nearby towns and city.

The above table reveals the problem and status of living of employees of organisation under study.

Designation – Executives:

Table 7 shows the designation wise distribution of the Executives selected as the sample among 150.

Majority of executives i.e.26.67 percent belonged to officer cadre. Another number i.e. 23.34 percent were from Asst. Manager Cadre.

Table - 7

Sl. No.	*Designation*	*Number*	*Percentage*
(a)	Senior Manager	10	6.66
(b)	Manager	34	22.66
(c)	Deputy Manager	31	20.67
(d)	Asst. Manager	35	23.34
(e)	Officer	40	26.67
	Total	**150**	**100**

Only 6.66 percent of respondents were holding the position of Senior Manager.

Thus majority of executives questioned were officers, Asst. Managers and Managers respectively.

Categories – Labourers:

Table – 8

Sl.No.	*Categories*	*Number*	*Percentage*
(a)	Highly Skilled	34	22.66
(b)	Skilled	60	40.00
(c)	Semi Skilled	36	24.00
(d)	Unskilled	20	13.34
	Total	**150**	**100**

The above table shows the categories-wise distribution of the labourers selected as the sample among 150.

Majority of the labourers i.e. 40 percent belonged to skilled category. Skilled category comprised of Fitters, Turners, and Electricians etc.

Another 24 percent of the labourers belonged to Semi-skilled category. Semi-skilled labourers were working as Operators, Weavers, Blenders, Spinners etc.

Highly skilled labourers were involved in job as Boiler and DJ Generation operator.

Reason for Joining Organisation:

Reason for joining the organisation reveals the attitude of individuals before seeking a job.

Table - 9

Sl. No.	*Reason for Joining Organisation*	*Executives* No.	*Executives* %	*Labourers* No.	*Labourers* %
(a)	Better Prospects	66	44	74	49.33
(b)	Better Salary	18	12	24	16.00
(c)	Prestigious Organisation	66	44	32	21.33
(d)	Job Security	-	-	20	13.33
	Total	**150**	**100**	**150**	**100**

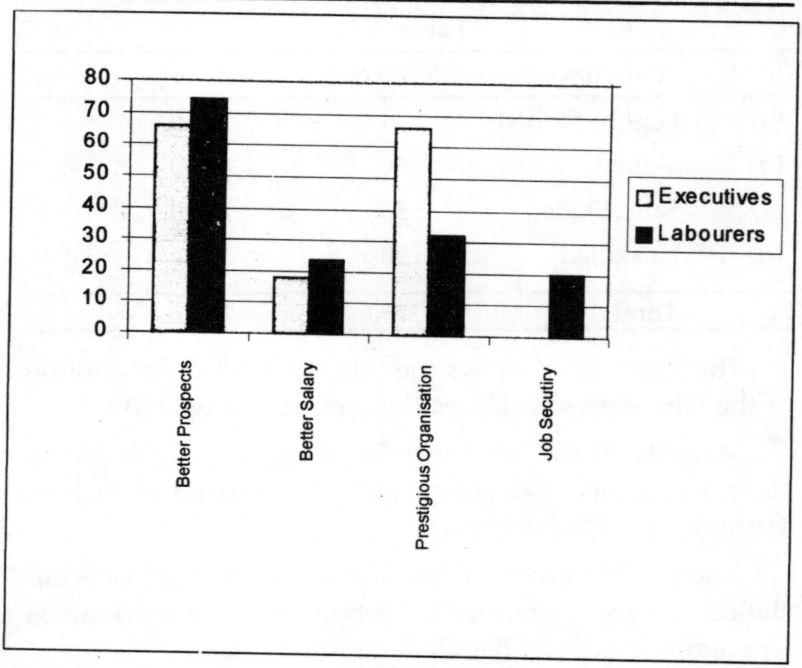

Graph - 3 : Reason for Joining Organisation

Before joining or seeking a job in any organisation, it becomes necessary for a person to think, " Why he is joining the organization", whether for good prospects or salary or prestigious organisation, so the researcher has tried to find out the reason for respondents joining the organisation.

Executives joined the organisation due to better prospects and prestigious organisation as revealed by 44 percent, while 12 percent of the executives joined the organisation due to better salary.

The sample thus shows that better future prospects and prestigious organisation were the two main reasons for joining the organisation both for executives and labourer. Salary, not being comparatively high was not the criteria for joining. Thus persons were more future oriented and the name of the organisation also played an important role in seeking a job.

Gender equity: Opinion of Employees

Table - 10

Sl. No.	*Opinion*	*Executives*		*Labourers*	
		No.	*%*	*No.*	*%*
(a)	Yes	132	88	108	72
(b)	No	-	-	-	-
(c)	Cannot Say	18	12	42	28
	Total	**150**	**100**	**150**	**100**

Gender equity is of great concern these days. The society is known to be male dominated. It was important to seek the employees opinion on this issue. All the respondents were male. 88 percent of executives opined that women should receive equal pay for equal work as compared to them, while 72 percent of labourers also opined the same.

Thus the concept that men are good at work and should

receive higher pay than compared to their counterparts women was not found in the organization. The concept of equal pay for equal work both for men and women, reveals that respondents treated women at par with them.

Acceptability of goals and belief defined by management:

Table - 11

Sl. No.	*Opinion*	*Executives*		*Labourers*	
		No.	*%*	*No.*	*%*
(a)	Yes	132	88	188	78.67
(b)	No	18	12	32	21.33
	Total	**150**	**100**	**150**	**100**

It was evident from the above table that executives and labourers were in favour of accepting the goals and belief defined by management.

As opined by 88 percent of executives and 78.67 percent of labourers, management should set up the goal and the employees must follow them.

The above table reflects the organisational commitment. It shows the degree to which an employee identifies with a particular organisation and its goals and wishes to maintain membership in the organisation.

This also reflects the job attitude of the respondents. Maximum percentage of executives and labourers showed a favourable attitude regarding acceptability of goals set up by management which also shows their job involvement, the degree to which the respondents participate in the goals and beliefs and consider their performance important to self –worth and for the development of organisation. Organisational commitment is a better predictor of job satisfaction because it is a more global and enduring response to the organisation as a whole as well as towards individual's job. As when the dissatisfaction spreads to the organisation itself the individuals are more likely to get dissatisfied with their jobs.

Role of job in raising the standard of living of the employees:

Table - 12

Sl. No.	*Opinion*	*Executives*		*Labourers*	
		No.	*%*	*No.*	*%*
(a)	Yes	126	84	98	65.33
(b)	No	24	16	52	34.67
	Total	**150**	**100**	**150**	**100**

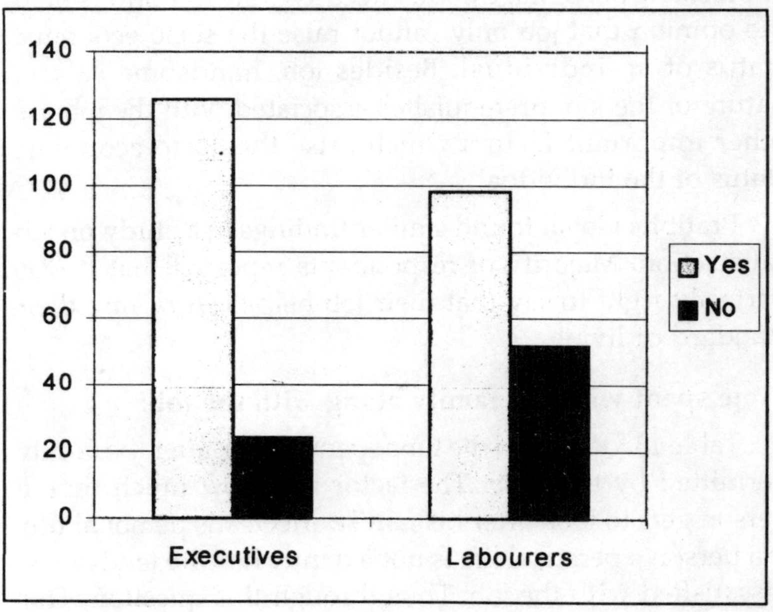

Graph - 4 : Role of Job in Raising Standard

Job satisfies a person who desires to work. It also brings money and status. This money helps him in maintaining or raising the standard of living. The extent upto, which a person's job helps in raising the standard of living, can be the factor determining his/her job satisfaction. Therefore the respondents were asked whether they felt that their job was helpful in raising the standard of living.

Maximum numbers i.e. 84 percent felt that it was perfectly right to say that their job helped in raising their standard of living. Only 16 percent reported that their job does not help in raising their standard of living. 65.33 percent of labourers felt their job certainly raised their standard of living and only 34.67 percent felt that it was wrong to say that their job enhanced their standard of living.

In the ultimate analysis it can be observed that an appreciable percentage of the executives and labourers held the opinion that job only cannot raise the socio-economic status of an individual. Besides job, handsome salary, nature of the job, prerequisites associated with the job are other important factors which raise the socio-economic status of the individual.

Pratibha Goyal found similar findings in a study on job satisfaction. Majority of respondents reported that it was perfectly right to say that their job helped in raising their standard of living.

Time spent with the family along with the job:

Table 13 focuses on the time spent to look after the family permitted by their job. The factor that how much time a person gets to look after his family affects his personal life. If a person's personal life is not a happy he/she tends to be dissatisfied with the job. Thus through this question. This table focuses on the time spent to look after the family permitted by their job. The factor that how much time a person gets to look after his family affects his personal life. If a person's personal life is not a happy he/she tends to be dissatisfied with the job. Thus through this question the researcher had asked the respondents i.e. executives and labourers to rate their opinion regarding time permitted by job to look after their family.

Table – 13

Sl.No.	*Responses*	*Executives*		*Labourers*	
		No.	*%*	*No.*	*%*
(a)	Mostly	72	48	75	50
(b)	Rarely	42	28	24	16
(c)	Always	36	24	51	34
	Total	**150**	**100**	**150**	**100**

Forty eight percent of executives reported that mostly they got enough time, 24 percent respondents said that they always got time to look after their family, while 28 percent of executives reported that very rarely they got time. 50 percent of labourers were of opinion that mostly they got enough time to look after their family, while 34 percent opined that always their job permitted to look after their family.

Thus we find that the respondents were satisfied with their job from the point of view of looking after their family, besides performing their job in the organisation effectively.

The wish of employees to get their wards employed in the same organization:

Generally the persons who are satisfied with their work and organisation and who like it much, are willing to get their wards also to be employed in the same organisation.

Table - 14

Sl.No.	*Opinion*	*Executives*		*Labourers*	
		No.	*%*	*No.*	*%*
(a)	Yes	36	24	66	44.00
(b)	No	48	32	40	26.67
(c)	Cannot Say	66	44	44	29.33
	Total	**150**	**100**	**150**	**100**

In the present case it was found that 44 percent of executives were not sure or were not able to answer the question. It seems that they were not willing express their wish. Another 32 percent did not wished to get their wards employees in the same organisation. Only 24 percent of executives agreed to employ their wards in the same organization

On the other hand 44 percent of labourers strongly wished to get their wards employed in the same organization, while 29.33 percent were not ready to answer or unable to express their willingness.Executives wished to educate their wards in order to get some better job. They felt that their present job did not give them sufficient status, money and work in textile industry. It leaves a bad impact on their health because of inhalation of cotton dust. The working conditions of the organisation were good but the executives believed that textile industry leaves some impact on the health. Labourers, on the other hand, were wishing to get their wards employed on the same organisations.

Thus in the final analysis it seems evident that executives being professionally educated wanted that their wards should work somewhere else because they saw limited scope in the organisation. On the other hand labourers who lacked reasonable background wanted to have their wards employed in the same organization, for they were suffering from the sense of insecurity.

Career prospects of employees in the organization:

Table – 15

Sl.No.	*Responses*	*Executives*		*Labourers*	
		No.	*%*	*No.*	*%*
(a)	Good	102	68	98	65.33
(b)	Average	30	20	20	13.33
(c)	Poor	18	12	32	21.34
	Total	**150**	**100**	**150**	**100**

It is evident from the above table that 68 percent of executives felt that there were good prospects in the organisation. Only 12 percent opined their prospects were poor in the organisation.

While 65.33 percent of labourers were of the opinion that their prospects in the organisation were good, other 21.34 percent opined about poor prospects in the organisation.

Better prospects in the organisation shows that the organisation provides intrinsic rewards for good performance, which motivates the employees to work sincerely. Organisation gives opportunity to complete a meaningful task, to interact with superiors in carrying out the job. The organisation also provides desired extrinsic rewards that provides greater security, make them feel a part of group, provides recognition and appreciates and allows the employees to grow and develop to their full potential.

Thus majority of respondents opined that organisation provides good prospects for their future development and betterment.

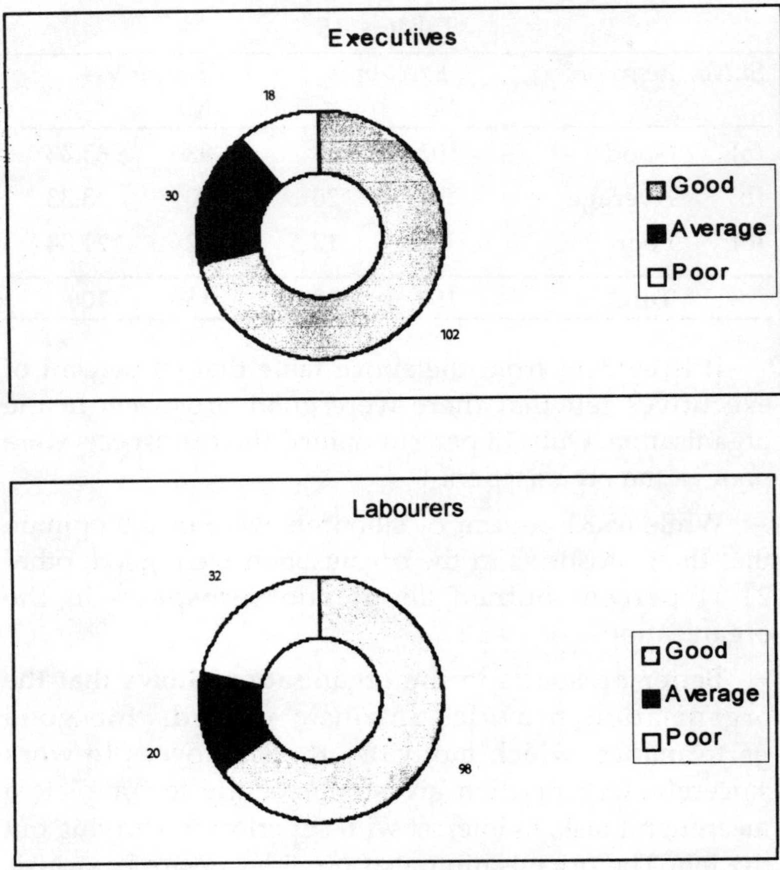

Graph -5 : Career Prospects

Choice of the job as revealed by employees:

Table – 16

Sl.No.	*Responses*	*Executives*		*Labourers*	
		No.	*%*	*No.*	*%*
(a)	Present Job	78	52	110	73.33
(b)	Another Job	48	32	30	20.00
(c)	Job in other Occupation	24	16	24	06.67
	Total	**150**	**100**	**150**	**100**

It is evident from the table that the respondents, if given a choice, would select the present job, as opined by 52 percent of executives and 73.33 percent of labourers. While 32 percent of executives and 20 percent of labourers were of the opinion that they would choose another job.

The above table makes it clear that the executives and labourers were satisfied with their present job. This job meets their level of satisfaction and provides them sense of achievement, power, status, affiliation, security which seems to be important enough to motivate the respondents to select the job. They act as hygiene factors. Factors such as company policy and administration, supervision and salary when adequate in job motivate the employees to select the present job. These hygiene factors also act as satisfiers. As shown in the present study the above factors were found to be responsible for selecting the present job.

Interpersonal relationship in the organization:

As regards interpersonal relationship among employees of the organisation, the above table shows that good interpersonal relationship exists in the organisation as opined by 80 percent executives and 88 percent labourers.

Interpersonal relationship provides efficient working and a good team work in the organisation.

Table – 17

Sl.No.	*Responses*	*Executives*		*Labourers*	
		No.	*%*	*No.*	*%*
(a)	Good	120	80	132	88.00
(b)	Average	24	16	10	06.67
(c)	Poor	06	04	08	5.33
	Total	**150**	**100**	**150**	**100**

Employees have understanding with their colleagues. An atmosphere of understanding exists and the respondents were assured of each others cooperation and thus they can fulfill their social needs and job related problem as they behave as members of group and their membership as group helps to shape their work behaviour and attitudes towards the organisation and the job.

Grievances of the employees:

Table - 18

Sl.No.	*Responses*	*Executives*		*Labourers*	
		No.	*%*	*No.*	*%*
(a)	Yes	66	44	56	37.33
(b)	No	84	56	94	62.67
	Total	**150**	**100**	**150**	**100**

Grievance implies dissatisfaction, or distress or grief caused due to employment. Prompt redressal of grievances is a must for creating good labour-management relations and promoting efficiency at the plant level. Employees of all types and at all levels develop grievances. Grievances

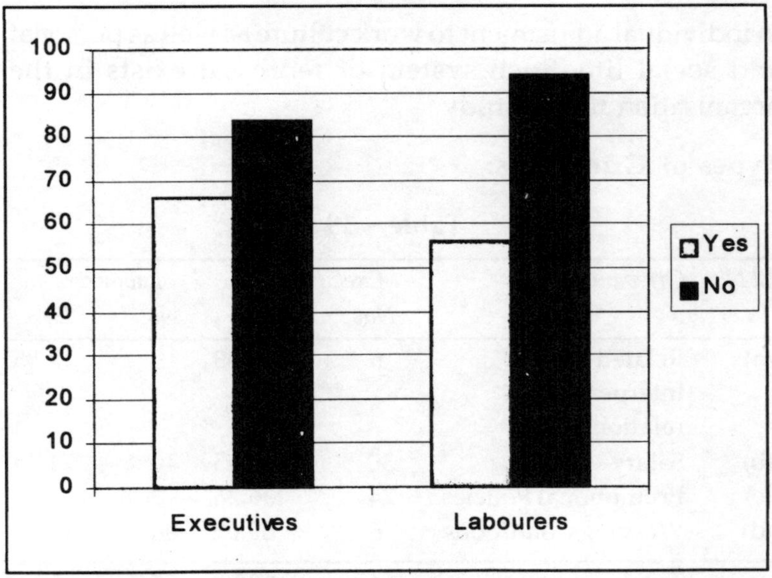

Graph - 6 : Grievances of the employees

are not only caused by management but can be due to general social condition and due to home environment. Grievances, if unsolved, gives rise to unhappiness, frustration, discontent, poor morale which leads to inefficiency of workers and low productivity. The above table shows 56 percent of executives did not had any grievances and 44 percent had grievances.

Labourers i.e. 62.67 percent opined that there were no grievances and remaining 37.33 percent had grievances relating to their salary and other job conditions.

Maximum percentage of the executives and labourers felt satisfied with their work and such occasion of grievance did not occur. Grievance rate is usually stated in terms of number of written complaints presented in the year per 100 employees.

The organisation has a grievance system, like counseling, which is a process of employees emotional release of their dissatisfaction. Such type of system plays an important role in individual adjustment to work culture as well as personal and social life. Such system of redressal exists in the organisation under study.

Types of Grievances:

Table - 19

Sl.No.	Grievances	Executives		Labourers	
		No.	%	No.	%
(a)	Related to Interpersonal relationship	6	09.09	10	17.85
(b)	Salary	30	45.45	40	71.44
(c)	Promotional Policies	24	36.36	-	-
(d)	Working Conditions	6	09.09	06	10.71
	Total	**66**	**100**	**56**	**100**

Grievances are human problems and are to be handled in a human way. Every worker presents his grievances to the employees and seeks their redressal. The management had to see the type of grievances and tries to settle the grievance so that the worker gets a sense of satisfaction. The employees defines and describes the nature of grievance at first and then makes a list of alternate solutions.

Only 66 executive and 56 labourers had grievances as seen in the previous table. These respondents were asked about the types of grievances they had.

45.45 percent executives opined that salary was their main grievance. Salary seems to be not sufficient to satisfy the executives. Salary is one form of motivation and has a direct bearing. It seems that the executives are those employees who were not getting wages or salary which was sufficient to satisfy their physiological needs. 36.36 percent executives had their grievance related to promotional policies. Promotional policies provide its employees with opportunity encouragement and career growth. It seems that inter-departmental disparity exists in the promotional policies of the organisation. Organisation does not provide equality of opportunities in promotion and an autocratic system is developing in the organisation. Only a few i.e. 9.09 percent had grievance related to interpersonal relationship and working conditions respectively.

The table shows that 71.44 percent labourers also had grievance related to salary, while 17.85 percent labourers had grievances relating to interpersonal relationship and only a handful i.e. 10.71 percent had grievance related to working condition. Labourers were satisfied with the promotional policies. From the above table it is clear that the nature of grievance as expressed by the majority of respondents i.e. 45.45 percent executives and 71.44 percent labourers were related to salary. Salary acted as a motivating factor. Salary policy should be checked and evaluated from time to time. Departmental ratings should be periodically checked to keep them up-to-date.

Relationship of employees with superiors:

Table - 20

Sl.No.	*Responses*	*Executives*		*Labourers*	
		No.	*%*	*No.*	*%*
(a)	Good	102	68	96	64
(b)	Average	48	32	54	36
(c)	Poor	-	-	-	-
	Total	**150**	**100**	**150**	**100**

The above table makes it clear that good relationship between respondent and superiors was existing in the organisation as shared by majority of executives i.e. 68 percent and 64 percent labourers respectively. The remaining 32 percent executives and 36 percent labourers were of the opinion to have average relations with superiors.

It is evident from the above data that proper interaction between superiors and subordinates exist in the organisation. As observed, apart from the formal hierarchy, the organisational structure also permits for good superior-subordinate relations. Good superior-subordinate relations can be maintained by proper interaction which is through conducting appraisal interviews, monthly meetings, discussing problems, solving their grievances, encouraging, motivating and appreciating them.

None of the respondents had poor relations with superiors. Thus it seems that above measures were taken by the organisation in order to maintain good relation among management and employees.

Good inter-personal relationship: a factor for effective functioning:

Table - 21

Sl.No.	*Responses*	*Executives*		*Labourers*	
		No.	*%*	*No.*	*%*
(a)	To a great extent	108	72	120	80.00
(b)	To some extent	24	16	28	18.67
(c)	Not at all	18	12	2	1.33
	Total	**150**	**100**	**150**	**100**

Respondents were asked whether they agreed that interpersonal relationship helps in effective working of organisation. 72 percent of the executives felt that interpersonal relationship among the employees is an important factor through which effective functioning of the organisation can be achieved. 80 percent of the labourers held the same opinion. Thus it can be concluded that interpersonal relationship is a key factor in any organisation for its effective functioning.

Team Work present in the organization:

Table - 22

Sl.No.	*Response*	*Executives*		*Labourers*	
		No.	*%*	*No.*	*%*
(a)	Substantial	30	20	22	14.67
(b)	Little	54	36	38	25.33
(c)	Very Much	66	44	90	60.00
(d)	None	-	-	-	-
	Total	**150**	**100**	**150**	**100**

Teamwork is understanding the interaction among the people. For teamwork there is a need for participation and involvement by all the members and understanding of all the members that they are engaged in a group task and not individual activities. Team work involves members getting together to take decision. Team work allows the employees to grow and contribute according to their abilities and potential. Team function is to modify, supplement, compliment and to achieve the desired goal.

Teamwork was also located at during the present study in the organization. 44 percent executives opined that very much teamwork was present in the organization, while 36 percent reported to have little teamwork. 60 percent labourers reported very much teamwork present and only 25.33 percent replied to have little teamwork.

Team building in order to diagnose the effectiveness of team and their inter-personal relationship must be improved in order to have more teamwork.

Good amount of teamwork existed as reported by majority of respondents in the organization.

Recognition of the work by superiors:

Table - 23

Sl.No.	*Response*	*Executives*		*Labourers*	
		No.	*%*	*No.*	*%*
(a)	Mostly	84	56	92	61.33
(b)	Occasionally	42	28	28	18.67
(c)	Rarely	18	12	18	12.00
(d)	Not at all	6	4	12	8.00
	Total	**150**	**100**	**150**	**100**

In any organization moral boosting and individual recognition are major factors which contribute to the higher productivity. In the present study a question was asked from the respondents as to how many times they were recognized for their good work. 56 percent of the executives were of the opinion that they were recognized mostly by the superiors for their good work. On the otherhand, 61.33 percent of the labours had the same opinion. Thus, it seems, organization rewards good work, which is very conducive for proper growth of an organization.

Fair treatment of the employees by the employers:

Table - 24

Sl.No.	*Response*	*Executives*		*Labourers*	
		No.	*%*	*No.*	*%*
(a)	Yes	126	84	118	78.67
(b)	No	-	-	-	-
(c)	Cannot Say	24	16	32	21.33
	Total	**150**	**100**	**150**	**100**

Table 24 makes it clear that the employees receive a fair treatment given by the employer. Majority of respondents i.e. 84 percent executives and 78.67 percent labourers were of the opinion that treatment by the employers is good.16 percent executives and 21.33 percent labourers were unable to answer or were not willing answer, as they reported - "cannot say."

Good treatment refers to an "Equal opportunity employer". The employer gives due regard to the interest of all parties i.e. employees, consumer, public and employees' expectations i.e. job security, security against old age sickness and accidents etc. The employer provides for the provision and proper facility like better working condition, welfare facilities, medical benefits, canteens, recreational facilities, rest rooms etc. Employees spend their life working for the organisation and in return they expect to be treated well. Fair treatment gives its employees a sense of belongingness, team work and sense of being appreciated, motivated towards their work, which in return increases the prosperity and production. Respondents, when probed, regarding what did they mean by fair treatment, referred to conducive work environment, involvement in the decision making, reasonable salary for work, benefits, opportunity for advancement and proper justice.

Participation of employees in management:

Table - 25

Sl.No.	*Response*	*Executives*		*Labourers*	
		No.	*%*	*No.*	*%*
(a)	Yes	132	88	98	65.33
(b)	No	18	12	52	34.67
	Total	**150**	**100**	**150**	**100**

Participation in Management is of great concern in todays Industrial setting. Workers' participation in Management is inevitable from economic, psychological and sociological point of view. It recognises employees' non-economic needs. The satisfaction of those needs through participation can help in raising the level of motivation. Sociologically the need for participation arises because modern industry is considered a social institution with the interests of capital owner, the employer, the community and the workers equally vested in it. Participation is considered to be highly effective, because it brings involvement which in turn brings commitment. Once commitment is achieved these, goals and objectives are achieved easily.

In the present study, high participation of employees was observed as opined by 88 percent executives and 65.33 percent labourers, while only 12 percent executives and 34.67 percent labourers opined that no participation for improvement was done.

Respondents felt that participation develops a team spirit in the organisation. The organisation involves workers representatives on the Board and in planning financial management and strategic planning. Participation in the organisation exists on all level. The executives were involved and consulted on such matter and work. However, final decision is always that of the Management, only advises of executives was taken. Thus it is clear that the concept stood for mere consultation or a procedure for co-thinking in the decision-making process or for co-determination.

The Industrial Policy Resolution in India (1956) also emphasises the need for workers participation in Management. In socialist democracy, labour is a partner in common task of development and participates in it with enthusiasm.

Promotional System in the organization:

Table - 26

Sl.No.	*Response*	*Executives*		*Labourers*	
		No.	*%*	*No.*	*%*
(a)	Seniority	-	-	60	40.00
(b)	Seniority cum Merit	120	80	80	53.33
(c)	Merit	30	20	10	6.67
	Total	**150**	**100**	**150**	**100**

Promotion involves a change from one job to another that is better in terms of status and responsibility. Promotion is advancement of an employee to a better job, greater responsibility, more prestige, greater skill and increased rate of pay or salary. Promotion is also an opportunity to the employees for recognition and to keep the morale of employees high.

An attempt has been made by the researcher to know the existing promotional system in the organisation. At the time the promotion policy is designed, its criteria or the basis for promotion is decided. 80 percent executives opined that seniority-cum-merit system was operational in the organisation. Only 20 percent executives opined that merit is considered at the time of promotion. 53.33 percent labourers expressed that seniority-cum-merit system of promotion exists in the organization. 40 percent labourers opined that seniority was considered at the time of promotion. Only a handful i.e. 6.67 percent labourers were of view that merit is considered at the time of promotion.

Thus it is clear that seniority-cum-merit system of promotion was in the organisation. Seniority-cum-merit is combination of two factors i.e. seniority and merit. Seniority means the length of service rendered for the organisation.

Merit rewards the employees on basis of his performance. Promotion based only on seniority or only on merit has its own demerits. Seniority is no indication of competence and young, competent people get frustrated and might leave the organization, on the other hand promotion by merit generates discontentment among senior employees. There can be also a scope for favouritism. Therefore, the system adopted by the organization, of promotion on the basis of seniority-cum-merit is more accurate. Such promotion policy considers the merit, potential and seniority of the employees.

Demotion System in the organization:

Table - 27

Sl.No.	*Response*	*Executives*		*Labourers*	
		No.	*%*	*No.*	*%*
(a)	Yes	84	56	108	72
(b)	No	66	44	42	28
	Total	**150**	**100**	**150**	**100**

Demotion is degrading of status, post, responsibility to lower authority. Demotions can be a result of Disciplinary Action or for poor performance and inefficiency of work by the employees. An attempt was made to know whether poor performance of employees results in demotion. 56 percent executives opined that inefficiency to work or poor performance results in their demotion while 44 percent executives reported that the employer took no such action.

72 percent labourers reported to be demoted on basis of poor performance, while 28 percent said no action was taken. It seems that labourers whose poor performance affects the productivity causing loss to the organisation were dealt with serious action in form of demotion. Thus the organisation has policies of reward-punishment. It

implies reward for the better performance, sincere work in the form of promotion and punishment for poor performance in the form of Demotion and Disciplinary action.

Attitude of Executives towards their Organisation:

Table – 28

Sl. No.	*Statement*	*Strongly Agree*	*Agree*	*Undecided*	*Disagree*	*Strongly Disagree*
1.	This company is good place to work.	54 (36%)	48 (32%)	18 (12%)	30 (20%)	-
2.	I can progress in this company, if I work hard.	60 (80%)	48 (32%)	18 (12%)	24 (16%)	-
3.	Benefits offered by company are fair.	18 (12%)	78 (52%)	54 (36%)	-	-
4.	Your job makes the best use of your abilities.	30 (20%)	66 (44%)	24 (16%)	-	-
5.	Your job is challenging, not burden.	78 (52%)	54 (36%)	18 (12%)	-	-
6.	You have trust and confidence in your boss.	90 (60%)	36 (24%)	18 (12%)	-	-
7.	You feel free to communicate to your boss.	78 (52%)	54 (36%)	18 (12%)	-	-
8.	You know what boss expects from you.	42 (28%)	102 (68%)	6 (4%)	-	-

(Table showing the percentage in parenthesis)

The respondents i.e. executives were further questioned through 5 point scale to ascertain their views towards their company where they were working. Among eight questions, which were asked some of them were positive, while others were negative, purpose was simply to know their present status in the organisation and how they rate their organisation. When the employees were asked regarding their company, majority 30 percent agreed that it was a good place to work. In another item when they were asked that hard work could lead them to progress, 80 percent agreed on this point. Similarly employees when asked regarding the benefits offered by the company, 52 percent agreed that they were reasonable.

Further, to assess the view of respondents regarding use of their abilities in the organization, 44 percent agreed that they were properly used, while 52 percent agreed that job was not a burden. Executives had trust and confidence in their bosses to the tune of 60 percent. They also felt themselves free to communicate with their bosses. Nearly 68 percent were aware of the expectations of their bosses from them.

Attitude of Labourers towards their Organisation:

A 5-point Scale was also used to seek the views of labourers towards their organisation. It was very important to know the attitude of labourers as well.

Eight statements were rated by the labourers which were the indicative of fact about their attitude.

Majority of respondents i.e. 36 percent agreed that organisation was good place to work. Another statement was asked to know whether hard work can lead to their progress - 48.33 percent agreed to it. A statement whether the benefits offered by the organisation were fair was also asked. 40 percent agreed to this statement, whereas a close

Table – 29

Sl. No.	*Statement*	*Strongly Agree*	*Agree*	*Undecided*	*Disagree*	*Strongly Disagree*
1.	This company is good place towork.	44 (30%)	54 (36%)	10 (6.67%)	36 (24%)	6 (4%)
2.	I can progress in this company, if I work hard.	44 (30%)	72 (48.33%)	24 (16%)	10 (6.67%)	-
3.	Benefits offered by company are fair.	14 (9.34%)	60 (40%)	18 (12%)	58 (38.66%)	-
4.	Your job makes the best use of your abilities.	40 (26.67%)	56 (37.33%)	-	24 (16%)	30 (20%)
5.	Your job is challenging, not burden.	48 (32%)	60 (40%)	24 (16%)	18 (12%)	-
6.	You have trust and confidence in your boss.	102 (68%)	22 (14.67%)	16 (10.66%)	10 (6.67%)	-
7.	You feel free to communicate to your boss.	68 (45.32%)	40 (26.67%)	22 (14.67%)	14 (9.34%)	6 (4%)
8.	You know what boss expects from you.	44 (30%)	94 (62%)	6 (4%)	6 (4%)	-

(Table showing the percentage in parenthesis)

number i.e. 38.66 percent disagreed on this point. Similarly employees were further asked regarding the use of their abilities - 37.33 percent agreed. 40 percent of the labourers agreed that job was challenging, not burden. Labourers expressed their trust and confidence in their bosses, as strongly agreed by 68 percent. 45.32 percent strongly agreed to communicate to their bosses freely. 62 percent of the labourers were aware of the expectations of their bosses.

Views of employees regarding their job :

Table – 30

Sl.No.	Response	Executives No.	Executives %	Labourers No.	Labourers %
(a)	Hate it	-	-	-	-
(b)	Like it	114	76	132	88
(c)	Dislike	-	-	-	-
(d)	Enthusiastic about it	36	24	18	12
	Total	**150**	**100**	**150**	**100**

Table 30 shows the view of employees towards their job. Majority of employees i.e. 76 percent of the executives and 88 percent of the labourers liked their job. The respondents thus rated their job and none of them hated the job. In the present study it was found that the employees liked their job, which is the indicator of the fact that the job was not boredom on the respondents. The job was challenging, not burden. The respondents enjoyed their work and liked their job.

Satisfaction of employees with their job:

Table - 31

Sl.No.	Responses	Executives No.	Executives %	Labourers No.	Labourers %
(a)	All the Time	60	40	80	53.33
(b)	Mostly	60	40	40	26.67
(c)	Rarely	30	20	30	20.00
(d)	Never	-	-	-	-
	Total	**150**	**100**	**150**	**100**

The above table reflects how often do the employees feel satisfied with their job. As opined by executives, 40 percent considered all the time and mostly their job satisfying. Majority of laboures i.e. 53.33 percent were of the opinion that they felt job satisfying all the time, while 26.67 percent of them responded to mostly their job as satisfying.

Job satisfaction all the time is indicator of the fact that factors such as nature of the work, supervisor, working conditions, pay benefits etc. were present in the job. These factors represent those job characteristics, which were used to assess job satisfaction. The above job dimensions were all job dimensions, which are equally important to all respondents in determining overall satisfaction with their jobs. Some respondents consider pay very important and working condition not so, for other it may be the reverse. Therefore, a combination of all measures of job dimension indicates the job satisfaction level.

Fair Pay :

Table - 32

Sl.No.	*Responses*	*Executives*		*Labourers*	
		No.	*%*	*No.*	*%*
(a)	Yes	66	44	60	40
(b)	No	84	56	90	60
	Total	**150**	**100**	**150**	**100**

It is evident from the above table that pay is not fair, as opined by majority of employees i.e. 56 percent executives and 60 percent labourers.

Thus it was clear that respondents believed their pay was comparatively low when compared with other organisations. Pay is one of the factors, which can be responsible for job satisfaction. Employees should receive sufficient money in form of salaries or wages to sustain himself and his dependents.

A handsome salary makes an employee satisfied with the relationship between his salary and the salary of other people in the same industry. It can be said in context to present study that the wage and salary administration policy of the organisation is not compensating employees for the services rendered by them to the organisation.

This factor is closely related to job satisfaction. Therefore the organisation under study must evaluate its wage policy from time to time to make them adequate, to meet current needs. The salary plan must also include an incentive system for efficient employees. The organisation must ensure higher pay to the employees who perform work at higher level of efficiency.

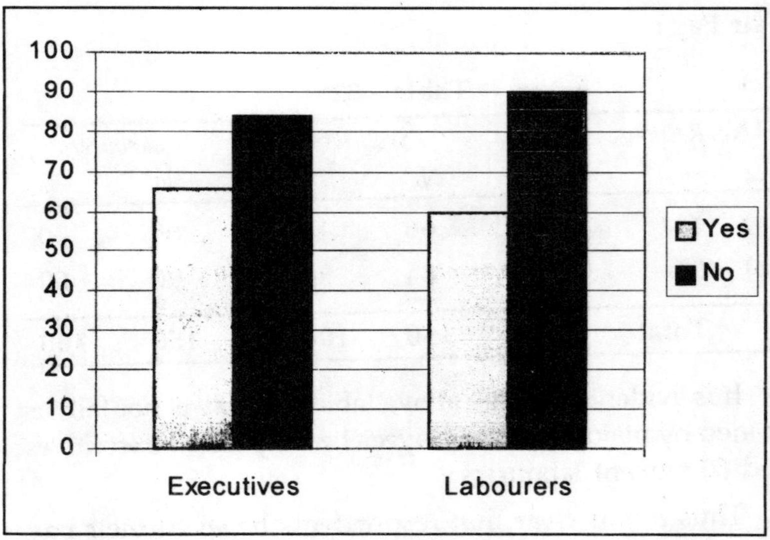

Graph - 7 : Fair Pay

Involvement in Decision Making :

Table - 33

Sl.No.	*Responses*	*Executives*		*Labourers*	
		No.	*%*	*No.*	*%*
(a)	Not at all	18	12	38	25.33
(b)	Usually	72	48	54	36.00
(c)	Occasionally	48	32	48	32.00
(d)	Fully Involved	12	8	10	6.67
	Total	**150**	**100**	**150**	**100**

Table 33 shows the involvement of Respondents in the Decision Making process. Decision-making is recognised as an important organisational and Management process for effective performance.

The researcher made an attempt to know how often were respondents involved in the decision making process. 48 percent of the executives and 36 percent of the labourers revealed that usually they were involved in the Decision Making process. 32 percent of executives and labourers opined that their involvement in the Decision-making was on occassions. The above data reveals that the involvement of respondents in Decision Making process exists in the organisation as revealed by majority of them.

On probing the respondents, they reported that their involvement was usually taken on the matters of their routine job, general job improvement techniques, setting of goals. The respondents also revealed that occassionally they were involved regarding decisions on their Salary, Incentives, Bonus and Company policies.

Level of satisfaction of employees regarding the cleanliness of the office :

Table – 34

Sl.No.	*Responses*	*Executives*		*Labourers*	
		No.	*%*	*No.*	*%*
(a)	Highly satisfied	42	28	38	25.33
(b)	Satisfied	102	68	110	73.33
(c)	Dissatisfied	6	4	2	1.34
(d)	Highly Dissatisfied	-	-	-	-
(e)	Undecided	-	-	-	-
	Total	**150**	**100**	**150**	**100**

The above table shows the level of satisfaction of respondents regarding the cleanliness of their office.

Majority of employees i.e. 68 percent executives and 73.33 percent of labourers were satisfied with the cleanliness of their office. On probing, the respondents revealed that dirt was removed daily by sweeping. The benches and chairs of the workrooms were also cleaned. Labourers, on investigating, also reported that floor of every workroom was cleaned at least once in every week by washing. On observation the researcher found that the ceilings, walls were well painted and the floors of the office as well as workshop were washed and cleared. Thus it can be said that the cleanliness was well maintained.

Level of satisfaction of employees regarding working conditions :

Majority of respondents i.e. 80 percent of the executives and 73.33 percent of labourers were satisfied with the working conditions provided by the organisation. Working conditions are necessary to make the employees work

Table - 35

Sl.No.	Responses	Executives No.	Executives %	Labourers No.	Labourers %
(a)	Highly satisfied	30	20	28	18.67
(b)	Satisfied	120	80	110	73.33
(c)	Dissatisfied	-	-	12	8.00
(d)	Highly Dissatisfied	-	-	-	-
(e)	Undecided	-	-	-	-
	Total	**150**	**100**	**150**	**100**

effectively. The respondents reported that the employer provides proper working conditions and a conducive work environment. On investigation, safe working conditions and healthy atmosphere was found in the organisation. Majority of the respondents told the researcher that proper lighting, cleanliness, drinking water and proper temperature were maintained in the organisation.

Level of satisfaction of the employees regarding loan facilities offered by the organisation :

Table - 36

Sl.No.	Responses	Executives No.	Executives %	Labourers No.	Labourers %
(a)	Highly satisfied	12	8	08	5.33
(b)	Satisfied	72	48	60	40.00
(c)	Dissatisfied	24	16	48	32.00
(d)	Highly Dissatisfied	42	28	34	22.67
(e)	Undecided	-	-	-	-
	Total	**150**	**100**	**150**	**100**

From the above table it can be seen that 48 percent of the executives were satisfied with the loan facilities rendered by the organisation whereas 28 percent of the executives were highly dissatisfied. The reasons for dissatisfaction were attributed to the fact that the executives were highly dissatisfied with the loans offered by the organization. They might have found the procedure of loan-advance as cumbersome and disgusting or it may be due to their incapability in returning the loan.

Another point, which was revealed in privacy, was that the management was giving loans to few select favourites only, not to everyone. In the labourer group, 40 percent were satisfied with the loan facilities availed by them, whereas 32 percent of them were dissatisfied. It seems that there were some loopholes in the loan procedure. Loan policy was not fair as considerable number of both groups were dissatisfied with the loan facilities offered by the organisation.

Level of satisfaction of the employees regarding the housing facilities provided by the organization :

Table – 37

Sl.No.	*Responses*	*Executives*		*Labourers*	
		No.	*%*	*No.*	*%*
(a)	Highly satisfied	24	16	10	6.67
(b)	Satisfied	36	24	18	12.00
(c)	Dissatisfied	54	36	60	40.00
(d)	Highly Dissatisfied	24	16	14	9.33
(e)	Undecided	12	8	48	32.00
	Total	**150**	**100**	**150**	**100**

The above table shows that 36 percent of the executives and 40 percent of the labourers were dissatisfied with the housing facilities. It was followed by 24 percent of the executives who had satisfaction towards housing facility.

About 32 percent of the labourers were undecided with this issue of housing facility. It was found during the present study that majority of respondents were living on rented accommodation, only a few of the respondents availed the housing facility provided by the organisation.

The respondents were dissatisfied with the housing facility because they felt that number of houses were comparatively less than the large working force. In similar study done by Pratibha Goyal on job satisfaction it was seen that majority of the respondents were satisfied with the housing facilities provided by the organisation. As compared in the present study, majority were dissatisfied with the housing.

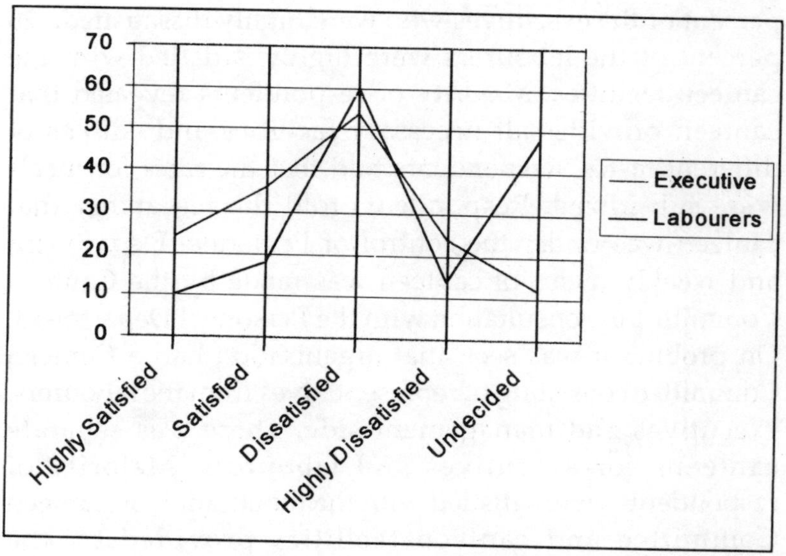

Graph - 8 : Satisfaction regarding the Housing Facilities

Level of satisfaction of the employees regarding the canteen facilities provided by the organization :

Table – 38

Sl.No.	*Responses*	*Executives*		*Labourers*	
		No.	*%*	*No.*	*%*
(a)	Highly satisfied	18	12	42	28.00
(b)	Satisfied	72	48	66	44.00
(c)	Dissatisfied	24	16	22	14.67
(d)	Highly Dissatisfied	36	24	20	13.33
(e)	Undecided	-	-	-	-
	Total	**150**	**100**	**150**	**100**

The above table indicates that 48 percent of the executives and 44 percent of the labourers were satisfied with the canteen facilities, which was followed by 24 percent of the executives who were highly dissatisfied. 28 percent of the labourers were highly satisfied with the canteen facilities. Majority of respondents revealed that canteen provides all necessary facilities and edibles of different tastes. Respondents told that the rates for meals were subsidized. Respondents told the researcher that canteen was under the control of Personnel Department and weekly menu of canteen was made by the Canteen Committee in consultation with the Personnel Department. On probing it was seen that organisation had a Canteen Committee consisting of representatives from the labourers, executives and management side. There was separate canteens for executives and labourers. Majority of respondents were satisfied with the functioning of Canteen Committee and canteen facilities provided by the organisation.

Level of satisfaction of the employees regarding the Training programmes:

Table – 39

Sl.No.	*Responses*	*Executives*		*Labourers*	
		No.	*%*	*No.*	*%*
(a)	Highly satisfied	24	16	48	32.00
(b)	Satisfied	84	56	60	40.00
(c)	Dissatisfied	30	20	20	13.33
(d)	Highly Dissatisfied	-	-	22	14.67
(e)	Undecided	12	8	-	-
	Total	**150**	**100**	**150**	**100**

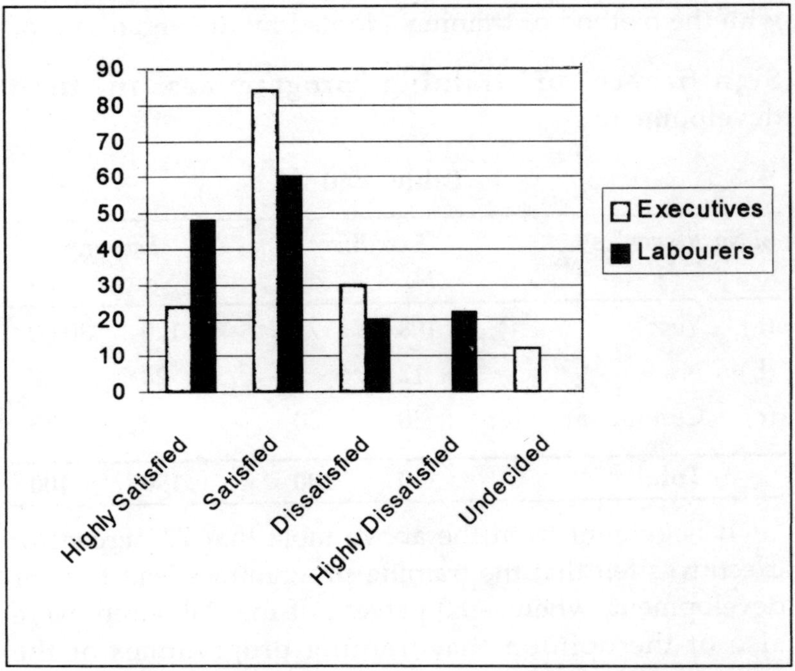

Graph - 9 : Satisfaction regarding Training Programmes

Training is the act of increasing the knowledge and skills of an employee for doing a particular job. The above table shows the satisfaction level of respondents relating to the training programmes. Majority of respondents were satisfied with the training programmes as opined by 56 percent of executives and 40 percent of the labourers, while 20 percent of the executives were dissatisfied with training programmes. On the other hand 32 percent of the labourers were highly satisfied by the training programmes conducted by the organisation. On probing the respondents the executives reported that the organisation adopted mainly on the job training method. Their immediate Bosses gave executives training at the work place. Labourers on the other hand revealed to have undergone vestibule training. Both the groups i.e. executives and labourers were satisfied with the method of training adopted by the organisation.

Significance of training programmes in their development:

Table – 40

Sl.No.	*Responses*	*Executives*		*Labourers*	
		No.	*%*	*No.*	*%*
(a)	Yes	108	72	120	80.00
(b)	No	12	8	28	18.67
(c)	Cannot say	30	20	2	1.33
	Total	**150**	**100**	**150**	**100**

It is evident from the above table that 72 percent of executives felt that the training programmes lead to their development, whereas 80 percent of the labourers were also of the opinion that training programmes of the organisation lead to their development. Majority of respondents felt that training programmes raise their skill levels and increase their versatility. The respondents reported the investigator that H.R.D. deptt. was imparting adequate training programme.

Communication System of the organization:

Table - 41

Sl.No. Responses	*Executives*		*Labourers*	
	No.	*%*	*No.*	*%*
(a) Downward communication	42	28	22	14.66
(b) Upward communication	30	20	28	18.67
(c) Horizontal communication	-	-	-	-
(d) Open communication	78	52	100	66.67
Total	**150**	**100**	**150**	**100**

It is evident from the above table that an open communication/direct communication exists in the organisation as opined by 52 percent of the executives and 66.67 percent of the labourers. On probing about open communication the respondents revealed to the researcher that they were free to communicate without any formal procedure to their superiors. They had direct communication with their immediate superiors and bosses. Such a communication system allows improving interaction among bosses and subordinates and also develops good interpersonal relationship among them.

Power and Authority of employees to take decision in routine work:

Table 42 shows the authority and power of the respondents to take decision regarding their routine work. 44 percent of the executives and 46.67 percent of the labourers opined that mostly they undertake the decision regarding their routine work.

Table - 42

Sl.No.	Responses	Executives No.	Executives %	Labourers No.	Labourers %
(a)	All the time	42	28	38	25.33
(b)	Mostly	66	44	70	46.67
(c)	Rarely	42	28	42	28
(d)	Never	-	-	-	-
	Total	**150**	**100**	**150**	**100**

On other land 28 percent of the executives were of the view that rarely do they enjoy the authority to take decisions, while 28 percent of the labourers also opined the same. Thus it can be said that neither executives or labourers had the freedom to take decision all the time.

Factors responsible for Job Satisfaction of employees:

Table - 43

Sl.No.	Responses	Executives No.	Executives %	Labourers No.	Labourers %
1.	Pay	22	14.66	24	16.00
2.	Security	62	41.33	58	38.66
3.	Working conditions	10	6.67	10	6.67
4.	Benefits	5	3.33	16	10.66
5.	Supervisors/Boss	8	5.33	7	4.66
6.	House of Work	4	2.66	6	4.00
7.	Opportunity for Advancement	30	20.00	18	12.00
8.	Management	6	4.00	8	5.33
9.	Communication	2	1.33	1	0.66
10.	Social aspects of Job	1	0.66	2	1.33
	Total	**150**	**150**	**150**	**100**

From the above table it can be seen that ten important factors which contribute to the job satisfaction were asked by the respondents i.e. executives and labourers. Majority 41.3 percent executives felt that job security was the major criteria of job satisfaction. Further 20 percent were of the opinion that there must be an opportunity to grow in the organisation.

On the other hand majority of the labourers 38.6 percent too had the same views and considered security one of the important factors for job satisfaction. Another dominant group 16 percent of the labourers considered pay as one of the major factor for job satisfaction. According to their view revision of pay from time to time and reasonable rise in the pay are important factors in job satisfaction.

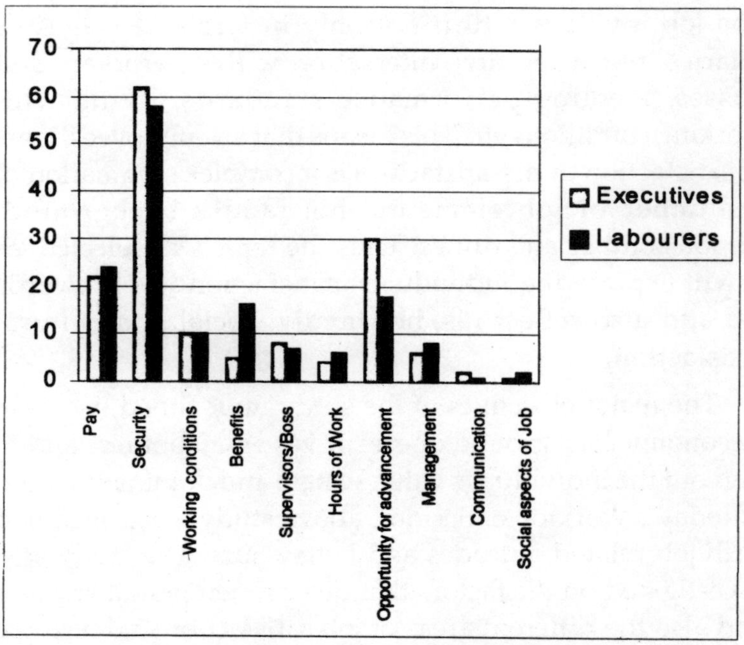

Graph - 10 : Factors of Job Satisfaction

VI

Conclusions and Suggestions

This study, which was author's doctoral dissertation, was designed to investigate "A Sociological study of Job satisfaction among Executives and Labourers with special reference to Raymond Ltd. in Chhindwara Distt. (M.P.)". The modern industrialization increased the expectations of people; their horizon of needs and this increased the level of satisfaction towards their job. Job satisfaction is referred to as "Individuals' general attitude towards his/her job." The job involves return not only in terms of wages or salaries, but it requires interaction with co-workers and bosses, meeting performance standards, living with working conditions etc. This means that an employees' level of satisfaction or dissatisfaction is a complex summation of a number of job elements, his family background, responsibilities and duties. Thus the topic was selected, as it will explore the individuals' satisfaction level towards job and also reflect his/her family, social and cultural satisfaction.

The major objectives of the study understood the socio – economic background of executives and labourers and to find out the individual's value system and dominant values in today's workforce. Besides, above study was concerned with job related attitudes and behaviours. The study also investigated on the factors that determined job satisfaction and also the different areas of job satisfaction and also the different areas of job satisfaction among respondents among executives and labourers in Raymond Ltd.

The study was carried out in Raymond Ltd. Sausar unit, Chhindwara. There were 300 employees viz. 150 executives and 150 labourers of Raymond Ltd. who provided the data. These respondents were selected on the basis of Stratified Random sampling.

CONCLUSIONS

Age of the Respondents: Majority of Executives and Labourers were in the age group between 31-40 years. It reflects the studied population was in younger age group.

Marital Status: As regards marital status, all the respondents were married.

Education Status: Most of the Executives and Labourers were reasonably educated. Majority of Executives (36%) were Post -Graduates. Labourers (80%) were Intermediate

Status of Job: All the Executives were on the permanent job. Majority of Labourers (66.67%) were on permanent job. Rest 23.33% Labourers were also on contract basis, which shows that organisation also had contract labour policy.

Period of Service: The period of service of the Executives was 5-9 yrs (64%), on the other hand majority of Labourers (61.33%) were in service from 10-14 years.

Monthly Salary: Majority of Executives (68%) was getting a monthly salary between 5001-8000. Labourers (81.33%) were drawing monthly salary ranging between 2000-5000.

Living Status: Majority of respondents i.e. 60% Executives and 80% Labourers were residing in the rented houses. Both the groups were facing problem of housing. The Organisation does not provide housing for all.

Reason for Joining Organisation: Better prospects and prestigious organisation were the main reason for joining the organisation as reported by majority of Executives (44%) and Labourers (49.33%)

Gender Equity: As regards gender equity, majority of respondents i.e. Executives (88%) and Labourers (72%) were of view that women should receive equal pay for equal work compared to them. Both the groups treated women employees at par with them.

Acceptability of Goals and Belief of the organisation: Majority of Executives (88%) and Labourers (78.67%) were in the favour of accepting the goals and belief defined by the organisation, thus reflecting the organisational commitment.

Role of Job in Raising standard of living: 84% of the Executives and 65.33% of Labourers felt that it was perfectly right that their job raises their standard of living.

Time spent with family: Majority of the respondents i.e. Executives and Labourers mostly got time to spent with their family permitted along with the job.

Wards employed in the same Organisation: 32% of the Executives did not wish to get their wards employed in the same organisation. They wanted to educate their wards and get some better job. But majority of Labourers (44%) strongly wished to got their wards employed in the same organisation.

Career Prospects: Majority of employees i.e. Executives (68%) and Labourers (65%) revealed that organisation provides good career prospects for their future development and betterment.

Choice of Job: Regarding selection of job, a large number of Executives (52%) and Labourers (73.33%) revealed to select the present job, which shows that organisation, meets their level of satisfaction and requirements.

extra resources to meet their increasing demands. Loan facilities as provided by the organisation are meager and they are given to selected few. Therefore there was a need to advance liberal loan facilities to the employees.

4. Major areas of grievance as reported by the respondents were Salary and Promotion policies. Any industrial organisation, which needs stability and peace, should consider these two areas dispassionately. Fair and time-bound promotional policy should be evolved. And revision of pay in a definite time frame should be formulated.

5. Labourers were interested regarding the employment of their wards in the same organisation in which they were working. This is the major area of job satisfaction, because workers realise a kind of social security that will enhance the productivity and output of the organisation.

6. The industrial atmosphere in the organisation which was studied revealed that there was lack of active participation in the decision making process. In order to have better industrial climate there is need of active participation of the employees at all levels, otherwise concept of participative management shall remain a distant reality.

7. As revealed by the study the Labourers were not in a very comfortable situation with regard to their economic status as compared to the Executives. Therefore it becomes the duty of employer that free and compulsory education should be provided to the wards of the Labourers. Organisation should open schools for the children of Labourers and provide scholarship and stipend to intelligent children. Even educated workers can work as volunteers in these schools.

8. Other benefits like Medical Services, Simplification of advance facilities, etc. be given. Welfare officer should be given a free hand in organization of welfare programmes, which in turn may help in increasing the better industrial atmosphere and level of satisfaction.

Bibliography

Abbas Ali, M., *Job Satisfaction and Work Motivation among Workers on Selected Industrial Undertakings in Hyderabad,* 1978.

Acharya, T.L., Philosophies of Lobour Welfare, *Indian Journal of Social Work,* Vol. 14, No. 1, 1953.

Aggarwal, V.K., and Mongia, T.N. ed., *Readings in Indian Labour and Social Welfare,* Atma Ram and Sons, Delhi, 1980.

Ali Mohammad, Abbas, *Job Satisfaction and Work Motivation among Workers in Select Industrial Undertakings in Hyderabad,* Osmania University, 1978.

Baldev, R., Determinants of Job Satisfaction Among Industrial Workers, *Vikalpa,* 5(1), January 1980.

Bhagoliwal, T.N., *Economics of Labour and Social Welfare,* Sahitya Bhawan, Agra, 1987.

Bhaskar, V. and Mongia, T.N. ed., *Readings in Indian Labour and Social Welfare,* 2nd edition , Delhi, Atma Ram & Sons, 1980.

Bhatia, S.K., *Personnel Management and Industrial Relations,* Deep and Deep Publications, New Delhi, 1983.

Bhatnagar, Deepak, *Labour Welfare and Social Legislation in India,* Deep and Deep Publications, New Delhi, 1985.

Bhatnagar, Deepti, *State and Labour Welfare in India,* Deep and Deep Publications, New Delhi, 1985.

Bhattacharya, Sisir, *The Welfare State in India: A Study,* ICSSR, New Delhi, 1981.

Bhattacharya, Vivek Ranjan, *Some Aspects of Social Security Measures in India,* (Unpublished), Indian Council of Social Sciences Research, New Delhi, 1982.

Blum, A.A. (Ed.), *International Handbook of Industrial Relations,* Greenwood Press Westport, Commedicut, 1981.

Blum M. and J. Ross, A Study of Employers' Attitude Towards Various Incentives, *Personnel,* Vol. 19, 1942.

Brown, J.A.C., *Social Psychology of Industry,* Harmondsworth, Middlesex, Penguin Books Inc., 1962.

Chopra, V.S., Strategies for Healthy Labour Management Relations, *Haryana Labour Journal,* Vol. 15, No. 3, July-Sept. 1984.

Das, N., *Industrial Labour in India,* Eastern Economy Pamphlets, 1951.

Devar, R.S., *Personnel Management and Industrial Relations,* Vani Educational Book, Delhi, 1985.

Davis, Keith, *Human Behaviour at Work,* Tata McGraw Hill, New Delhi, 1977. *Encyclopedia of Social Sciences,* Vol. XV, 1935.

Gangrade, K.D., How Employees View Their Work, *Indian Journal of Industrial Relations,* Vol. 2, No. 1, July, 1966.

Ganguli, T., Group Participation as an Effective Technique to Improve the industrial Workers' Attitude and Morale, An Experiment, *Indian Journal of Psychology,* Vol. 33, 1958.

Giri, V.V., *Industrial Relations,* Asia Publishing House, Bombay, 1955.

Giri, V.V., *Labour Problems in Indian Industry,* Asia Publishing House, Bombay, 1972.

Goyal, R.C., *Problems of Personnel Management and Industrial Relations in Indian,* National Publishing House, New Delhi, 1972.

Gujral, B.B., Labour Welfare Personnel and its Framing, *Indian Journal of Social Work*, Vol. 10, No. 3, 1949.

Gupta, O.P., *Commitment to Work of Industrial Workers*, Concept Publishing House, New Delhi, 1981.

Harrell, Thomas W., *Industrial Psychology*, Oxford and IBM Publishing Company, London, 1976.

Hoppock, R.R., *A Handbook of Industrial Welfare*, 1955.

Hoppock, R., *Job Satisfaction*, New York, Harper, 1935.

Kabra, R.N., *Industrial Relations Scene*, The Need for the Hour, Personnel, 1979.

Khaleque, A. and Chaudhary, Nilima, Job Facts and Overall Job Satisfaction of Industrial Mangers, *Indian Journal of Industrial Relations*, 20(i), July, 1984.

Khan, A.F., Managerial Responses to Social Responsibility: A Challenge, *Indian Management*, 20(9), September 1981.

Khanna, H.L., India's Labour Welfare Policy and Five Year Plans, *Commercial Law Gazette*, 6(32), 9 September 1983.

Kornhauster, Arthur, Psychological Studies of Employee Attitudes, *Journal of Consulting Psychology*, 1944.

Kudchedkar, L.S., *Aspects of Personnel Management and Industrial Relations*, Tata McGraw Hill Publishing Co. Ltd., New Delhi, 1979.

Kulkarni, M.R., *Industrial Development*, National Book Trust, New Delhi, 1971.

Lakshami, N.A., What is Job Satisfaction, *Hindu*, 12 May 1980 p. 7, 1-4.

Lalvani, K.C., *Labour Welfare in India*, Artha Vanijay, Calcutta, 1987.

Locke, E.A., The Nature and Causes of Job Satisfaction in M.D. Dunnette (Ed.), *Handbook of Industrial and*

Organisatonal Psychology, Chicago Rand McNally, 1976.

McGregor, Douglas, *The Human Side of Enterprise*, Tata McGraw-Hill Publishing Company Ltd., Bombay, 1971.

Monappa, Arun, *Industrial Relations*, Tata McGraw Hill Publishing Company Ltd., New Delhi, 1985.

Mongia, J.N. (Ed.), *Readings in Indian Labour and Social Welfare*, Atma Ram & Sons, New Delhi, 1981.

Mukherjee, R.K., *Labour and Planning*, Allied Publishing, Bombay, 1964.

Narchal, Renu, Job Satisfaction: Some Correlates, *Productivity* 25(3), Oct.-Dec. 1984.

Pestonjee, D.M., *Organisational Structure and Job-Attitudes*, Minerva Associates, Calcutta, 1973.

Prasad, L.M., Motivational Dynamics in Indian Industry, *Indian Journal of Labour Economics*, 25(4), January, 1988, pp. 78-87.

Raman Rao, A.V., *Essays on Indian Labour*, Popular Prakashan, Bombay, 1965.

Rama Rao. K., *Labour Management Relations in Cotton Textile Industry in Andhra Pradesh*, Tirupati, 1989.

Rawat, B.D., *Labour Welfare In India: Problems and Prospects*, RBSA Publishers, Jaipur, 1988.

Roy, S.K., and Menon, A. Sree Kumar, (Ed.), *Motivation and Organisational Effectiveness*, Shri Ram Center for Industrial Relations, New Delhi, 1974.

Rudravasvraj, M.N., *Personnel Administration Practices in India*, Vaikunth Mehta, National Institute of Cooperative Management, Poona, 1969.

Saxena, R.C., *Labour Problems and Social Welfare*, Educational Publishers, Meerut, 1981.

Scott, *Personnel Management, Principles, Practices and Point of View,* Tata McGraw Hill, New Delhi, 1977.

Seligram, Edwin, R.A., and Alvin Johnson (Ed.), *Encyclopedia of Social Sciences,* Vol. 15, McMillan, New York, 1962.

Sen, A.K., *Indian Labour Legislation,* World Press, Calcutta, 1964.

Seth, N.R., *Industrial Sociology in India, A Book of Readings,* Allied Publishers, New Delhi, 1982.

Sharma, B.R., *Indian Industrial Workers,* Vikas, Delhi, 1974.

Shrimali, P.D., *Industrial Relations in Cotton Textile Industry in Kanpur, A Study Based on Case Studies,* Mimeo, Labour Research Committee, Lucknow University, 1970.

Singh, A.P., and Srivastava, A.K., Occupational Level and Job Satisfaction, *Journal of Public Relations,* 19(2), May 1975.

Singh, V.B., *An Introduction to the Study of Indian Labour Problems,* Shiv Lal and Co. Agra, 1967.

Singh, V.B., *Climate for Industrial Relations,* Allied Publishers, New Delhi, 1968.

Singh, V.B., (Ed.), *Patterns of Social Security,* Asia Publishing House, 1960.

Sinha, R.P., Study of Job Satisfaction Among Workers of A Steel Industry, *Indian Journal of Labour Economics,* 25(4), January 1983.

Srivastava, A.K., Motivation and Job Satisfaction in Satisfaction in Indian Industries, *Indian Journal of Labour Economics,* 26(1), April-July, 1983.

Srivastava, A.K., *Job Motivation,* Deep and Deep Publications, New Delhi, 1984.

Steers and Porter, *Journal of Applied Psychology,* Vol. 76, 1979.

Tandon, B.K., *Collective Bargaining and the Indian Scene,* Sultan Chand and Sons, Delhi, 1973.

Tata, N.H., Philosophies of Labour Welfare, *Indian Journal of Social Work,* Vol. 14, No. 1, 1953.

Verma, Pramod, *Management of Industrial Relations,* Vora Publishers, Ahmedabad, 1979.

Zaheeruddin, *Labour Welfare and Employment Conditions in India,* Deep and Deep Publications, New Delhi; 1985.

Index